Widows, Heirs, and Heiresses in the Late Twelfth Century:

The *Rotuli de Dominabus et Pueris et Puellis*

MEDIEVAL AND RENAISSANCE
TEXTS AND STUDIES

VOLUME 308

Widows, Heirs, and Heiresses in the Late Twelfth Century:

The *Rotuli de Dominabus et Pueris et Puellis*

Edited and Translated
by

JOHN WALMSLEY

ACMRS
(Arizona Center for Medieval and Renaissance Studies)
Tempe, Arizona
2006

Library of Congress Cataloging-in-Publication Data

Rotuli de dominabus et pueris et puellis de XII comitatibus. English.
  Widows, heirs, and heiresses in the late twelfth century : the Rotuli de
dominabus et pueris et puellis / edited and translated by John Walmsley.
    p. cm. -- (Medieval and Renaissance texts and studies ; v. 308)
  Includes bibliographical references (p.) and indexes.
  ISBN-13: 978-0-86698-353-2 (acid-free paper)
  ISBN-10: 0-86698-353-8 (acid-free paper)
1. Great Britain--History--Henry II, 1154-1189--Sources. 2. Great Britain--
Genealogy. I. Walmsley, John, 1937- II. Title. III. Series: Medieval &
Renaissance Texts & Studies (Series) ; v. 308.

  DA200.R68 2006
  942.03'1--dc22

                                                              2006005847

∞
This book is made to last.
It is set in Adobe Caslon Pro,
smyth-sewn and printed on acid-free paper
to library specifications.
Printed in the United States of America

CONTENTS

for SUSAN
(1950-2004)
In memoriam

ACKNOWLEDGMENTS

The motivation behind a new edition and translation of the twelfth-century *Rotuli de Dominabus et Pueris et Puellis* lay in the need of a growing number of students, at undergraduate and postgraduate levels, to obtain access as fully and accurately as possible to the sources of medieval history in general and women's history in particular. Moreover, even if there were no shortcomings in the two previous editions of these records in 1830 and 1913, there would still be a considerable benefit to having the original text published in parallel with the translation for pedagogic reasons. My first and principal acknowledgment therefore is to the many students who have demanded such access and to those who have persisted in asking questions about the female half of the population. In particular, I should like to express my gratitude and indebtedness to the late Gabrielle McManus of Macquarie University, who worked on these records with me in the preparation of her thesis on twelfth-century women, which sadly she was unable to finish.

I am indebted to Macquarie University for providing a research grant, which enabled me to take up a Visiting Fellowship at Clare Hall, Cambridge University, in the summer of 2002. To the Governing Body and Staff of Clare Hall I extend my thanks for providing a congenial and collegial environment in which to work and hospitality second to none. Likewise I thank the Staff of Cambridge University Library, the British Library, and the Public Record Office in London, especially Dr. David Crook.

I should also like to thank Dr. Marjorie Chibnall of Cambridge University for her encouragement over a long period of time and for reading and commenting on an early draft of this work. Thanks too are due to my anonymous readers, who have helped in improving the presentation and reducing errors to a more acceptable level, and to Dr. Jane Walmsley for her help in the more technical aspects of production.

Finally, of course, there is the debt to Susan, my late wife, my severest critic and best friend, who originally turned my thoughts to exploring in greater detail the history of the other half of the human race.

John Walmsley
Macquarie University
Sydney, 2006

North

R. Humber

● Lincoln

LINCOLNSHIRE

North Sea

The Wash

RUT-
LAND

Oakham ●

NORFOLK

Norwich ●

NORTHAMPTONSHIRE

CAMBRIDGESHIRE

HUNTS
Huntingdon ●

Northampton ●

● Bedford

Cambridge ●

SUFFOLK

BEDFORD-
SHIRE

Buckingham ●

Ipswich ●

BUCKINGHAMSHIRE

HERTFORDSHIRE

ESSEX

Hertford ●

Chelmsford ●

MIDDLESEX

London

R. Thames

Scale: 20   40   60   80   100   Km

The Twelve Counties of the *Rotuli de Dominabus et Pueris et Puellis*

INTRODUCTION

At first sight it might seem superfluous to produce another edition of a document that has already been published twice. The *Rotuli de Dominabus et Pueris et Puellis* of 1185 was first published in 1830 by Stacey Grimaldi of the British Museum and again in 1913 by John Horace Round.[1] In the belief that the original twelfth-century manuscript had been lost, Grimaldi prepared his edition from a seventeenth-century transcript by Sir Simonds D'Ewes.[2] Fortunately, by Round's time the *Rotuli* had resurfaced and was printed anew as a supplement to the pipe roll for 1184–1185. Both books are now difficult to obtain, especially for general students of history. Furthermore, for those without Latin there has to be a strong reliance on extracts, abstracts, and comments in a plethora of recent works on women's history,[3] demographic history, and economic history,[4] some of whose authors have not looked at the document as a whole, let alone the original manuscript. This edition therefore is accompanied by a parallel translation and numbered entries to facilitate referencing and cross-referencing.

---

[1] London, PRO, E. 198/1/2. S. Grimaldi, ed., *Rotuli de Dominabus et Pueris et Puellis de Donatione Regis in XII Comitatibus* (London, 1830); J. H. Round, ed., *Rotuli de Dominabus et Pueris et Puellis de XII Comitatibus* [1185], Publications of the Pipe Roll Society 35 (London, 1913): hereafter Round, *RD*.

[2] As part of Sir Simonds D'Ewes, *Historica Monumenta Diversa*: British Library, Harleian MS 624, fols. 148a–160a and 215b–217a. The transcript was certified by Sir Simonds D'Ewes and Roger Dodsworth on 3 May 1643.

[3] See especially E. Amt, *Women's Lives in Medieval Europe: A Sourcebook* (New York, 1993); J. Ward, *Women of the English Nobility and Gentry* (Manchester, 1995); P. Coss, *The Lady in Medieval England* (Stroud, 1998); and M. Johns, *Noblewomen, Aristocracy and Power in the Twelfth-Century Anglo-Norman Realm* (New York and Manchester, 2003).

[4] The most thorough demographic study of the *Rotuli* is in J. S. Moore, "The Anglo-Norman Family: Size and Structure," *Anglo-Norman Studies* [hereafter *ANS*] 14 (1992): 153–96. Other studies of a demographic and economic kind to draw upon the *Rotuli* include D. Herlihy, *Medieval Households* (Cambridge, MA, 1985); RaGena C. DeAragon, "Dowager Countesses, 1069–1230," *ANS*, 17 (1995): 87–100; and H. E. Hallam, "Farming Techniques: Eastern England," in *The Agrarian History of England and Wales*, vol. 2 *(1042–1350)*, ed. J. Thirsk (Cambridge, 1988), 272–312.

The *Rotuli* consists of twelve small rolls, or rotulets, the tops of which have been sewn together to form a descending booklet rather than a continuous roll. Although the membranes are reasonably consistent in width, measuring for the most part 15–20 cm., they vary considerably in length, from 6 cm. for the Middlesex fragment (roll 12) to 65 cm. for Norfolk (roll 6). Clearly the rolls have been brought together in this way for preservation purposes. They do not form a complete record, and whole (second) rolls for Suffolk and possibly Cambridgeshire seem to be missing. Indeed, for a while in the seventeenth century the second roll for Buckinghamshire with the entries for Rutland and Huntingdonshire on the dorse side were thought to be lost, which is why they appear separately in Sir Simonds D'Ewes's transcript.[5] The manuscript is then a very incomplete and uneven record written up in a number of similar hands by clerks attached to the royal justices. The first and last rolls (those for Lincolnshire and Middlesex) are written up in one hand; the remainder have at least two, with a tendency to cramping at the foot of the membrane.

The twelve counties covered by the rolls are, in order of appearance, Lincolnshire, Northamptonshire, Bedfordshire, Buckinghamshire, Rutland, Huntingdonshire, Norfolk, Suffolk, Hertfordshire, Essex, Cambridgeshire, and Middlesex (see Map, p. v). Entries are made hundred by hundred and in the case of Lincolnshire by wapentakes. In all, there are some 228 entries unevenly divided among the twelve counties and the hundreds or wapentakes within them. There is only one entry for Middlesex, two for Huntingdonshire, three for Rutland, five for Hertfordshire, and eight for Bedfordshire, whereas there are 42 entries for Lincolnshire, 40 for Essex, 37 for Norfolk, 32 for Buckinghamshire, 23 for Suffolk, 20 for Northamptonshire, and 15 for Cambridgeshire. The fuller titles given in endorsements within the rolls themselves for Buckinghamshire and Cambridgeshire give the clearest indication of the contents, viz.: *Rotulus de dominabus et puellis que sunt de donatione domini regis, et de pueris qui sunt in ejus custodia, in Bukinghamsire* and *Rotulus de viduis et puellis que sunt in donatione domini regis et de pueris qui sunt in ejus custodia in Cantebrigesire* — that is, rolls relating to ladies and girls in the gift of the king and boys who are in his wardship.

The entries collected together county by county are the result of the response of the hundred courts to a special enquiry into the property and status of widows and wards on estates held directly of the Crown, whether by knight service or by serjeanty, and on estates held more indirectly as a result of ecclesiastical vacancies, such as those at York and Lincoln, and escheats, such as those of the

---

[5] Harl. MS 624, fols. 215b–217a. Because Grimaldi failed to number this roll there appear to be only eleven rather than twelve rolls in his edition. Therefore Norfolk to Middlesex appear as rolls 5–11 instead of 6–12.

honours of Giffard, Haughley and Peverel. The enquiry was conducted by four named itinerant justices whilst on eyre in 1185.[6] Some of the results of the work of these four justices — Hugh of Morwich, Ralph Murdac, William Vavassor, and Master Thomas of Hurstbourne — are to be seen in the pipe roll for the following year, where they are identified as the justices for eleven of the twelve counties in the *Rotuli*.[7] Essentially what is recorded is the testimony (*verumdictum*) of the hundred court, although the term *verumdictum* is used with any frequency only under Essex (5 times) and once for Hertfordshire. The name of the hundred or wapentake is included inconsistently and, generally speaking, applies only to the entry or two immediately following the hundredal rubric.

In the decades of reconstruction following Stephen's reign the need to ensure an adequate flow of income and services from royal and non-royal sources alike was undoubtedly a prime incentive for this sort of enquiry. W. L. Warren and others have done much to bring to life the creativeness as well as the continuities involved in tracking down and making good actual and potential losses to the crown, whether through the restoration of the general eyres with a wider range of investigative powers or through a programme of restocking royal manors.[8] More acutely and specifically, it has been argued that the nature of patronage itself changed dramatically in the course of Henry II's reign, from one that depended on the use of the royal demesne and other estates that fell into the crown's hand through escheats and forfeitures to one that depended more on the fuller exploitation of feudal rights, especially those of wardship and marriage.[9] One of the means and results of this was the more thorough and more methodical investigation into the status of widows and wards that seems to have been

---

[6] For a short description of this procedure see A. L. Poole, *From Domesday Book to Magna Carta*, 2nd ed. (Oxford, 1955), 400.

[7] *Pipe Roll 32 Henry II*, xxiii. A very good example of the connection between the *Rotuli* of 1185 and the pipe roll for 1186 are the entries relating to Robert fitz Robert de Setvans in Essex. The *Rotuli* records that his property at Wigborough would be worth £16 if fully stocked, and the pipe roll for 1186 shows the sheriff duly accounting for £16 at the Exchequer: *Rotuli*, entry no. 203, and *Pipe Roll 32 Henry II*, 12.

[8] W. L. Warren, *Henry II* (Berkeley and Los Angeles, 1973), esp. pt. 2, "The Government of England." More recent works include R. Mortimer, *Angevin England 1154–1258* (Oxford, 1994), chap. 2, "The King's Government," and E. Amt, *The Accession of Henry II in England: Royal Government Restored 1149–1159* (Cambridge, 1993), esp. chaps. 8 and 10.

[9] J. E. Lally, "Secular Patronage at the Court of Henry II," *Bulletin of the Institute of Historical Research* [hereafter *BIHR*] 49, no. 120 (1976): 159–84. For an important modification to this view, which takes into account the empowerment of women at this level, see Johns, *Noblewomen*, chap. 9.

initiated c. 1176 with the Assize of Northampton.[10] Its earliest and most concrete achievement was what has come down to us as the *Rotuli de Dominabus et Pueris et Puellis*.

As with Domesday Book exactly a century earlier, much of the enquiry is concerned with the potential values of properties, as well as the current state of affairs and the recent record of usage and profits under custodians and farmers of the estate. Unlike Domesday Book, however, there exists no more or less set formula or list of questions posed by the commissioners, despite Round's assertion that the twenty-third *capitulum* of the instructions issued to itinerant justices in 1194 were "precisely such instructions as must have been given for the inquest to which the returns are found in the *Rot. de Dom*."[11] However that may be, whether one looks backward from Roger of Howden's long list of 1194 or forward from the brief instructions of the Assize of Northampton in 1176, it is clear that we are dealing with an isolated working document, a *rotulus justiciarum* (or *rotuli justiciarum*), which has managed to survive after the matter recorded in it had been dealt with elsewhere: for example, in the pipe rolls of the Exchequer. In this sense the *Rotuli* appears to be a precursor of the *veredicta* of the general eyre, of which so few survive, and then only from 1235.[12] The possibility that there had been a similar enquiry eight years earlier, in 1177, the year after the Assize of Northampton, is suggested by the frequent references in the *Rotuli* to the "last eight years."[13]

The properties and personnel of the *Rotuli* vary widely, from estates worth only a few shillings or a few marks per annum to some worth £40 (four instances) and, in one case, potentially more than £40 (entry no. 11, the Paynel fee), from wives of serjeants and lesser knights to countesses (Margaret of Brittany and Richmond, Matilda and Bertrada of Chester, Juliana of Norfolk, and Eva, countess of Ireland). Allowing for a certain amount of overlapping, most of the 228 entries (128) deal with the property of widows, 81 deal with male heirs, 16 with heiresses, and six cannot be ascertained. Because of the appearance of some of these widows and wards (both heirs and heiresses) more than once in different hundreds and different counties, the *Rotuli* in fact deal with fewer individuals — and therefore fewer families — than may seem the case at first sight: viz. 99 widows,

---

[10] Clause 9 of the Assize of Northampton included the task of enquiring into "women who are in the gift of the king": D. C. Douglas and G. W. Greenaway, eds., *English Historical Documents 1042–1189* (London, 1968), 413.

[11] *Pipe Roll 32 Henry II*, xxiii–xxiv.

[12] D. Crook, *Records of the General Eyre*, Public Record Office Handbook 20 (London, 1982), 34–35.

[13] Nos. 30, 46, 60, 76, 103, 139, 145, 162, 163, and 167.

60 male heirs, and about a dozen heiresses and groups of heiresses.[14] Many of the male heirs and widows are dealt with in consecutive entries (viz. 5/6, 38/39, 43/44, 72/73, 77/78, 84/85, 92/93, 121–123, 140/141, 185–187, and 205/206), but clearly, when the properties involved were in different counties and hundreds, related wards and widows are not grouped in this way (e.g., 16 and 20; 53 and 82; 49, 105, and 140; 50 and 153; 213 and 215; 178, 182, and 225).

The usefulness of this record as a source for genealogical, personal-, and place-name studies is well appreciated.[15] Its most thorough use in recent times, however, has been demographic;[16] its most neglected, surprisingly, has been economic. For example, it is not mentioned at all as a source for the history of prices in *The Cambridge Agrarian History of England and Wales*, nor has a great deal been done with it in the context of estate values, which were almost its raison d'être. The actual values of stocked estates are given for about 60 percent of properties, and only about half of these are followed up with potential values if full stocking were to take place.[17] Other areas of investigation to which a study of the *Rotuli* could well contribute include inheritance issues and the origins and role of the custodians placed in charge of widows, heirs, and heiresses, and their estates. More too needs to be done in the context of women's studies. As E. van Houts has put it: "A study of this fascinating document as a source of women's history remains to be written."[18] It is to be hoped that this small volume will promote this and other causes.

---

[14] In many cases the number of daughters is not stated, and there is reference to one niece. The number of widows is considerably fewer than the 128 suggested by E. van Houts in *Memory and Gender in Medieval Europe* (London, 1999), 82, a figure probably derived from Moore, "The Anglo-Norman Family," in which he talks about 128 reconstructed families (see 157 *et passim*).

[15] Coss, *The Lady in Medieval England*, 26. Most, but not all, of Round's identification of personal- and place-names can be accepted without question. Discrepancies have been indicated in the footnotes.

[16] See n. 4 above.

[17] This is the most obvious corrective to the generalisation that "The greater part of the estates were understocked": Grimaldi, *Rotuli de Dominabus*, iv, and to Hallam's suggestion, based on two entries for Lincolnshire (nos. 30–31), that "farming (in that county) was not all that it should have been": *The Agrarian History of England and Wales*, 2: 307–8.

[18] van Houts, *Memory and Gender in Medieval Europe*, 82, although a recent work that has gone a long way towards addressing this issue is Johns, *Noblewomen*, chap. 9, "Royal Inquests and the Power of Noblewomen: The *Rotuli de Dominabus et Pueris et Puellis de XII Comitatibus* of 1185," 165–93, and Appendix 2, "Noblewomen in the *Rotuli de Dominabus*," 231–45.

Notes to Text and Translation

1. In the Latin text pounds, shillings, and pence are represented by *l.*, *s.*, and *d.*; in the English translation by £, s and d. *Ob* for *obolus* = ½d. Marks, with a value of 13s 4d, are indicated in the Latin text with *m.*, but are presented in full in the translation.

2. Hundreds and wapentakes recorded in the original MS are indicated in bold type in both the Latin text and the translation.

3. Hundreds and wapentakes subsequently identified are indicated in normal type and placed in round brackets in the translation only.

4. *uxor*, *que fuit uxor*, and *uxor que fuit* are translated throughout as "widow."

5. *villa* and *manerium* are translated as "vill" and "manor," despite the fact that where they appear together in the same entries (nos. 122 and 162) they clearly mean the same thing.

6. *nepos* and *nepta/neptis* have been translated as "nephew" and "niece," although it is recognised that both can refer to grandchildren.

7. The punctuation and capitalisation of the Latin text has been modernised.

8. Conjectural missing words and letters are placed within square brackets in the Latin text.

Widows, Heirs, and Heiresses in the Late Twelfth Century:

The *Rotuli de Dominabus et Pueris et Puellis*

ROTULI DE DOMINABUS ET PUERIS ET PUELLIS

London, PRO E198/1/2
[Rot. 1.]

De dominabus et pueris et puellis de Lincolnscira

1. Uxor Euerardi de Ros, que fuit filia Willelmi Trussebut, est de donatione Domini Regis, et .xxxiiij. annorum, et habet .ij. filios; primogenitus est .xiij. annorum. Et terra ejus est in custodia Ranulfi de Glamuill' (*sic*). Et terra dicte domine in Stroweston' quam habet in dote, valet annuatim .xv. *l.* cum instauramento .ij. carrucarum et .c. ovium et iij. porcorum et .j. equi, nec potest plus valere.

2. Matillis de Seinliz, que fuit filia Roberti filii Ricardi et mater Willelmi de Albeneio, est de donatione Domini Regis, et est .lx. annorum. Terra sua in Hungerton' et in Wiuewelle, valet .x. *l.* cum instauramento .ij. carrucarum et .viij.xx. ovium et .ij. equorum et .v. porcorum, nec potest plus valere.

3. Filie Mathei de Neuill' sunt de donatione Domini Regis, et in custodia Hugonis de Creissi elapso .j. anno a Nativitate Domini; et prius his .viij. annis, fuerunt in custodia Roberti de Stuteuill', cum terra earum quam habent in Denton', que valet .viij. m. per annum: et tantum inde recepit annuatim Robertus de Stuteuill' .viij. annis, et nihil amplius, et eandem firmam recepit Hugo de Creissi elapso .j. anno a Nativitate Domini. Et si appositum esset instauramentum .j. carruce et .c. ovium, dicta terra valeret annuatim .viij. *l.* Etas dictarum puellarum ignoratur a juratoribus, quia sunt in transmarinis partibus.

ROLLS CONCERNING LADIES, BOYS, AND GIRLS

[Roll 1.]

Concerning ladies, boys and girls of Lincolnshire

(Winnibriggs Wapentake)

1. (Rose) the widow of Everard de Ros, daughter of William Trussebut, is in the Lord King's gift.[1] She is 34 years of age and has two sons. The firstborn is 13 and his land is in the wardship of Rannulf Glanvill. The said widow's land in Stroxton, which she has in dower, is worth £15 per annum with stock of 2 plough-teams, 100 sheep, 3 pigs, and one horse, and it cannot be worth more.

2. Matilda of Senlis, daughter of Robert fitz Richard and mother of William d'Aubigny, is in the Lord King's gift and is 60 years of age. Her land in Hungerton and Wyville is worth £10 with stock of 2 plough-teams, 160 sheep, 2 horses, and 5 pigs, and it cannot be worth more.[2]

3. The daughters of Matthew de Neville are in the Lord King's gift and (were in) the wardship of Hugh de Cressy for a year ending at Christmas (1184).[3] For eight years before that they were in the wardship of Robert de Stuteville, together with their land in Denton, which is worth 8 marks per annum: and Robert de Stuteville received as much, and no more, each year.[4] Hugh de Cressy received the same farm for the one year ending at Christmas. And if stock of one plough-team and 100 sheep were added the said land would be worth £8 per annum. The jurors do not know the girls' ages because they are overseas.

---

[1] Her mother was Aubrey de Harcourt, aged 50: entry no. 57. Rose's elder son was Robert de Ros: J. W. Clark, ed., *Liber Memorandorum Ecclesie de Bernewelle* (Cambridge, 1907), 48. See also C. T. Clay, *Early Yorkshire Charters* 10 (Wakefield, 1955), esp. 8–11.

[2] Round, *RD*, 1, n. 2, identifies this Matilda with Matilda *de Beaverio* in the Suffolk entry (no. 161), not under Norfolk, as his footnote states. She was the widow of William d'Aubigny of Belvoir. See also J. H. Round, *Feudal England* (London, 1964), 360, 432.

[3] Hugh de Cressy was a member of the king's household from 1171 to 1189: Lally, "Secular Patronage," 182. See also Warren, *Henry II*, 309.

[4] See no. 174, which refers to the death of Robert de Stuteville (1183).

Langho Wapentak'

4. Thomas de Arci, filius Thome de Arci, est in custodia Domini Regis, et est .xviij. annorum. Thomas de Arci, pater ejus, obiit die Sancti Swithuni .v. annis elapsis. Willelmus Basset saisivit totam baroniam ejus in manum Domini Regis, et tradidit eam Michaeli de Arci, cum hoc instauramento, scilicet, .viij. bobus, .lx. ovibus, .v. marcatis bladi. Michael de Arci tenuit dictam terram Noctone et Dunstone per annum et dimidium; primo anno recepit inde .xij. *l.* de assiso redditu, et de perquisitionibus .xxviij. *s.*; dimidio anno sequenti recepit .c. *s.* et .xij. *s.* et .iij. *d.* de assiso redditu, et de perquisitionibus .xx. *s.* Postea recuperavit Alina, uxor Thome de Arci, custodiam filii sui et terre cum dicto instauramento et blado, et tenuit terram per annum, et in fine anni obiit. Et postea fuit saisita dicta terra in manum Domini Regis, et justicie Domini Regis tradiderunt eam custodiendam Michaeli de Arci et Hereueo de Ossint', qui eam tenuerunt per annum et dimidium; et primo anno post obitum dicte Aline receperunt .xx. *l.* et .viij. *d.* de assiso redditu, cum instauramento .viij. boum et .ij. equorum, et de perquisitionibus .vj. *l.* Sequenti anno receperunt .x. *l.* et .iiij. *d.* de assiso redditu, et de perquisitionibus .iij. *l.* Dicta terra valet annuatim sine instauramento et sine dominico .xvj. *l.* Et si dominicum esset instauratum .iiij. carrucis et .cccc. ovibus et .xx. vaccis et .ij. tauris et .xx. porcis, posset tota terra valere .xxvij. *l.* Preterea Willelmus Basset cepit de dicta terra primo anno post obitum Thome de franco plegio .j. *m.*; secundo anno .x. *s.*; tertio anno .viij. *s.* De catallis Michaelis de Arci cepit Willelmus Basset .xiij. boves et .ij. equos, .lxxiij. oves et .xv. porcos, et bladum waignagii unius carruce et .dccc. turvas turbarum et .j. mullonem feni, que appreciata fuerunt .xv. *l.* et .xiiij. *s.* Dicta terra fuit .iij. annis in manu Domini Regis, et Willelmus Basset cepit inde singulis annis .iij. *l.* de communi auxilio, scilicet, .ix. *l.*

5. Bilingeia est de archiepiscopatu Eboracensi et est in manu Domini Regis cum herede, scilicet, filio Petri de Bilingeia, qui est .xv. annorum. Dicta villa reddebat tempore Petri .vj. *l.* et .x. *s.* et .viij. *d.*, et sine dominio; et si dominium esset instauratum .ij. carrucis et .xx. vaccis et .ij. tauris et .c. ovibus et .x. porcis et .j. verre, dicta terra valeret .xj. *l.* et .xviij. *d.* Post obitum Petri exaltavit archiepiscopus dictam villam ad .xvj. *l.*; et ideo, ut aiunt juratores, est villa destracta et homines

Langoe Wapentake

4. Thomas Darcy, son of Thomas Darcy, is in ward to the Lord King and is 18 years of age. Thomas Darcy senior died five years ago on St Swithun's Day.[5] William Basset[6] seized the whole of his barony into the Lord King's hand, and handed it over to Michael Darcy with the following stock: viz. 8 oxen, 60 sheep, and grain to the value of five marks. Michael Darcy held the said land of Nocton and Dunston for one and a half years. In the first year he received £12 from fixed rent and 28s from perquisites (of court); in the following half-year he received 112s 3d from fixed rent and 20s from perquisites. Afterwards Aline, Thomas Darcy's widow, recovered wardship of her son and his land with the above stock and grain and held the land for a year, and at the end of that year she died.[7] Then the said land was seized into the Lord King's hand and the justices handed the wardship of it over to Michael Darcy and Hervey of Horsington, who held it for one and a half years. In the first year after Aline's death they received £20 0s 8d from fixed rent, with stock of 8 oxen and 2 horses, and £6 from perquisites. In the following (half) year they received £10 0s 4d from fixed rent and £3 from perquisites. The said land is worth £16 per annum, not counting stock and demesne. And if the demesne were stocked with 4 plough-teams, 400 sheep, 20 cows, 2 bulls, and 20 pigs the whole estate could be worth £27. Moreover, in the first year after Thomas's death William Basset took one mark from frankpledge, in the second year 10s, and in the third year 8s. From Michael Darcy's stock William Basset took 13 oxen, 2 horses, 73 sheep, 15 pigs, grain of one plough-team, 800 turves of peat, and one stack of hay, which were worth £15 14s. The said land was in the Lord King's hand for three years and William Basset took £3 per annum from it in common aid, that is £9 (in total).

5. Billinghay belongs to the archbishopric of York and is in the Lord King's hand, together with the heir, the son of Peter of Billinghay, who is 15 years of age. In Peter's day the said vill used to return £6 10s 8d, not counting the demesne; and if the demesne were stocked with 2 plough-teams, 20 cows, 2 bulls, 100 sheep, 10 pigs, and one boar the said land would be worth £11 1s 6d. After Peter's death the archbishop revalued the vill to £16. In this way, according to the jurors, the vill and

---

[5] 2 July 1180.

[6] William Basset was sheriff of Lincolnshire from Easter 1177 to Easter 1185. For the history and influence of the Basset family see especially W. T. Reedy, ed., *Basset Charters c. 1120–1250*, Pipe Roll Society, 85 n.s. 1 (London, 1995), viii–xviii.

[7] Aline accounted for £200 for the wardship of her sons and their land in 1182: *1182 Pipe Roll*, 57. In 1183–1184 she still owed £157 13s 4d: *Pipe Roll 30 Henry II*, 18. For the early history of the Darcys of Nocton see *The Complete Peerage*, 4: 50, note c. For more on Thomas Darcy see no. 32.

destracti. Dicta villa fuit in manu Domini Regis .iij. annis et dimidio, et homines reddiderunt firmam Radulfo de Huntendon' per preceptum custodum archiepiscopatus, scilicet, Laurentii archidiaconi Bedeford et magistri Rogeri Arundel et Willelmi le Vauassur, scilicet, primo anno xv. *l.* et xvj. *s.*, et de .j. libero homine quedam calcaria deargentata, et de quodam alio .j. libram piperis, et de reragio archiepiscopi, .vj. *s.* et .viij. *d.* Secundo anno reddiderunt eidem .xvj. *l.*; et similiter calcaria et .j. libram piperis. Tertio anno .ix. *l.* et .iij. *s.* et .iiij. *d.*, et similiter calcaria et .j. libram piperis; dimidio anno .xxvj. *s.* et .viij. *d.* et similia calcaria et .j. libram piperis. Et Willelmus Basset vicecomes habuit de dicta villa dum fuit in manu Domini Regis de auxilio vicecomitis .lxx. *s.*

6. Uxor que fuit Petri de Bilingeia est de donatione Domini Regis, et Willelmus Talun habet illam; sed nescitur a juratoribus si desponsaverit eam vel non.

7. Filius Alberti Gresle, quem habuit de filia Thome Basset, est .xj. annorum, et in custodia Gilleberti Basset per preceptum Domini Regis. Terra sua in Swineshaued die mortis Alberti Gresle valuit .c. et .ij. *s.* sine instauramento quod est in manerio, scilicet, .xxij. boves et .ij. vacce et .j. taurus et .iiij. juvence et .ij. vituli et .lx. porci. Thomas Basset recepit inde .ij. firmas, scilicet, .xlij. *s.* Gillebertus Basset post mortem Thome recepit inde .iiij. firmas, scilicet, .lxxvij. *s.*; et .xxx. *s.*[i] de fabis et frumento; et de placitis .xxix. *s.* Post tradiderunt Gilebertus Basset et Radulfus Gibewin dictam terram ad firmam Alano de Wichetoft et Johanni clerico et Waltero de Herlaue et Johanni filio Astun pro .xviij. *l.* preter maram et pomerium, cum predicto instauramento et cum omnibus exitibus terre; et de his .xviij. *l.* recepit Gilebertus Basset. iiij. *l.* et .x. *s.* Postea tradiderunt Gilebertus Basset et

---

[i] Round, *RD*, 4, has extended to "solidatas," but equally it could be "solidos."

its men were impoverished and distressed. The said vill has been in the Lord King's hand for three and a half years,[8] and the men rendered the farm to Ralph of Huntingdon by order of the archiepiscopal custodians, namely Lawrence, archdeacon of Bedford, master Roger Arundel, and William Vavassor:[9] viz. in the first year £15 16s, a pair of silver-plated spurs from a certain freeman, one pound of pepper from another, and 6s 8d from the archbishop's arrears; in the second year, the same men rendered £16, and similarly spurs and one pound of pepper; in the third year, £9 3s 4d, and again spurs and one pound of pepper; in the half-year, 26s 8d and a similar pair of spurs and one pound of pepper. And William Basset, the sheriff, had 70s in sheriff's aid from the said vill while it was in the Lord King's hand.

6. Peter of Billinghay's widow (Alice) is in the Lord King's gift, and William Talun is living with her, but it is not known by the jurors if he married her or not.[10]

(Beltisloe Wapentake)

7. The son of Albert Grelley (Robert), whom he had by the daughter of Thomas Basset, is 11 years of age and he is in the wardship of Gilbert Basset (son of Thomas Basset) by order of the Lord King. At the time of Albert Grelley's death his land in Swinstead was worth 102s, not counting the stock which is on the manor, viz. 22 oxen, 2 cows, one bull, 3 heifers, 2 calves, and 60 pigs. Thomas Basset received two (annual) farms from there, amounting to 42s. After Thomas's death, Gilbert Basset received three farms from there, viz. 77s, 30 shillings from beans and wheat, and 29s from the pleas (of court). Afterwards Gilbert Basset and Ralph Gibewin handed over the said land at farm to Alan of Wichetoft, John, the clerk, Walter *de Herlaue* and John fitz Aston for £18, except for the marsh and orchard, together with the aforesaid stock and all proceeds from the land. Of this £18 Gilbert Basset received £4 10s. Afterwards Gilbert Basset and Ralph Gibewin

---

[8] The archbishop of York had died in November 1181. Three and a half years would bring the dating of the *Rotuli* to May 1185.

[9] One of the four justices in eyre. The other three were Hugh de Morwich, Ralph Murdac, and Master Thomas of Hurstbourne: see endorsement to Roll 7. These four officials appear to have acted together at other times: Warren, *Henry II*, 295. With the title of *magister* Thomas of Hurstbourne appears to have been one of the few justices to have had university training. All but Thomas of Hurstbourne acted as custodians of estates and/or wards of the very estates they were investigating.

[10] Four years later the marriage was still the subject of enquiry: *Pipe Roll 1 Richard I*, 68, where the widow is identified as Alice, wife of Peter of Billinghay. She paid 20s to have her land pending the outcome of the enquiry.

Radulfus Gibewin Nigello filio Alexandri et Roberto de Burun dictam villam per preceptum Domini Regis pro .xx. *l.* per annum; et ipsi retinuerunt[ii] eam jam per .ij. annos et .iiij. partes anni per predictam firmam .xx. *l.*, et non potest terra plus valere.

Marginal note: d.[iii]

8. Margareta Comitissa, soror Regis Scottorum, est de donatione Domini Regis, et est .xl. annorum, et habet terram in Chircheton' Wapentak', que data fuit sibi in dote pro .xxj. *l.* Anno quo fuit in manu Domini Regis reddidit .xxiij. *l.* de quibus Reinerius, senescallus Ranulfi de Glamuill', recepit ad opus Domini Regis .c. et .xv. *s.* dum fuit in manu Domini Regis, scilicet, de quarta parte .j. anni. Modo terra est in manu comitisse, que apposuit postea .iiij. carrucas, et possent apponi .cc. oves.

9. Uxor Roberti filii Hugonis de Tateshale est de donatione Domini Regis, et neptis Comitis Gileberti de Gant: et ignoratur de terra ejus, quia nichil habet in wapentak' de Hornecastro, cujus hoc est verumdictum.

[ii] Round, *RD*, 4: "tenuerunt."

[iii] This is the first of many such marginal notes, which are indicated inconsistently in Round's edition; this one is omitted. Its meaning is far from clear. One possibility is that "d" (*debet*) refers to an amount owing. I owe this suggestion to Dr. David Crook.

gave the said vill to Nigel fitz Alexander[11] and Robert de Burun by order of the Lord King for £20 per annum; and they have held it now at the aforesaid farm of £20 for two and three-quarter years, and the land cannot be worth more.[12]

(*Marginal note*: d.)

(Kirton Wapentake)

8. Countess Margaret, sister of the King of Scots,[13] is in the Lord King's gift and is 40 years of age, and she has land in Kirton Wapentake, which was given to her in dower for £21. In the year in which it was in the Lord King's hand it returned £23 of which Reiner, Rannulf Glanvill's steward,[14] received 115s for the Lord King's use while it was in the Lord King's hand, that is for the fourth part of one year. Now it is in the countess's hand, who subsequently placed 4 plough-teams there, and 200 sheep could be added.

(Horncastle Wapentake)

9. The widow of Robert fitz Hugh of Tattershall is in the Lord King's gift and she is a niece of Earl Gilbert of Gant. Nothing is known about her land because she has nothing in Horncastle Wapentake, whose testimony this is.[15]

---

[11] Nigel fitz Alexander became sheriff of Lincolnshire in 1185, succeeding William Basset. He is described by Round (*RD*, 45–46, n. 3) as "a rising official." For further references to Nigel fitz Alexander see nos. 15, 28, 49, 105, 111, 140, and 141.

[12] For further entries relating to the Grelleys, see nos. 15, 28, 109, 111, 130, 138, 158, and 197. Entries 111 and 158 reveal that Albert Grelley's son (Robert) had three sisters.

[13] She is also styled countess of Richmond (no. 12) and countess of Brittany (no. 216). She appears again as Countess Margaret in no. 160. Her age is given as 40 here and in no. 160, but 30 in no. 216. She was the widow of Conan, count of Brittany (d. 1171), then of Humphrey de Bohun, a steward of Henry II (d. 1181). See Johns, *Noblewomen*, 71, 165, *et alibi*.

[14] This is Reiner of Waxham, who was in Rannulf's service from at least 1171. He was a close ally and friend who went on crusade with Rannulf in 1190 and for whom Rannulf tried (unsuccessfully) to arrange a marriage: R. Mortimer, "The Family of Rannulf Glanville," *BIHR*, 54 (1981), 11–14.

[15] See nos. 17 and 21. No. 17 has a marginal note referring to Horncastle Wapentake.

10. Filius Gileberti Hansard est in custodia Domini Regis cum terra sua de Sucheleseia cum omnibus pertinentiis a .xv. diebus post festum Sancti Michaelis, quia Rogerus de Muntbegun noluit recipere homagium Gileberti Hansard. Bladum quod ibi invenit senescallus Rogeri de Muntdegun valuit .xxiiij. *l.* et .vj. *s.* in frumento et ordeo et fabis et avena et brasio. Dictus Rogerus habuit saisinam dicti manerii usque ad .xv. dies ante Natale, et recepit de firma .iij. *m.* et dim.; et dictus senescallus asportavit de minutis utensilibus ad valentiam .iij. *m.* Exinde fuit in manu vicecomitis usque ad .iij. septimanas ante Pentecosten, qui nihil inde recepit. Postea fuit in manu Hugonis de Morewich et adhuc est; qui inde recepit de firma .lj. *s.* et .iij. *d.* Dicta terra valet sine instauramento .viij. *l.* et .j. *m.* que reddenda est canonicis de Turnet' pro dimidia carrucata terre, quam Gilebertus Hansard tenuit de illis in vita sua; et cum instauramento .iiij. carrucarum et .cc. ovium et .v. vaccarum et .j. tauri valeret terra .xvj. *l.* et .j. *m.* Heres est in custodia matris, que est de donatione Episcopi Dunelmensis: et hec terra est instauranda.

Marginal note: Instaur'.

11. Filius Petri Pounel, qui est .iiij. annorum, est in custodia Domini Regis, cum terra sua in Westrase; et fuit a festo Sancti Martini usque nunc; et in custodia vicecomitis per preceptum Domini Regis, qui de firma anni preteriti cepit inde per Willelmum filium Siward' .xix. *l.* et .iiij. *s.* et .viij. *d.* et *ob.* et de firma hujus anni .xiij. *l.* et xvii. *s.* et x. *d.* Dicta terra valet annuatim .xxxviij. *l.* et .j. *m.* et .x. *m.* domine de Merchez, cum instauramento quod ibi est, scilicet, .vj. carrucis, .cccc. ovibus, .xxx. vaccis, .ij. tauris, .x. suibus, .ij. verribus et .j. avero. Et si adderentur .x. vacce et .cc. oves que desunt, dicta terra valeret per annum .xlij. *l.*: et hec terra precipitur instaurari.

Uxor que fuit Petri Pounel est de donatione Domini Regis.

Marginal note: Instaur'.

(Walshcroft Wapentake)

10. The son of Gilbert Hansard is in ward to the Lord King, together with his land of South Kelsey and all its appurtenances, since the fifteenth day after Michaelmas,[16] because Roger de Montbegon refused to receive the homage of Gilbert Hansard. The crops which Roger de Montbegon's steward found there were worth £24 6s in wheat, barley, beans, oats, and malt. Roger had possession of the said manor until 15 days before Christmas, and received 3½ marks from the farm; and the above steward carried off minor equipment to the value of 3 marks. Afterwards it was in the sheriff's hand until three weeks before Pentecost, and he received nothing from it. Then it was in Hugh de Morwich's hand and it still is, and he received 51s 3d from the farm. The said land without stock is worth £8 and one mark, which (mark) ought to be paid to the canons of Thornton for the half-carrucate of land that Gilbert Hansard held from them in his lifetime.[17] With stock of 4 plough-teams, 200 sheep, 5 cows, and one bull the land would be worth £16 and one mark. The heir is in the wardship of his mother, who is in the gift of the bishop of Durham. This land is to be stocked.

(*Marginal note*: to be stocked)[18]

11. The son of Peter Paynel, who is 4 years of age, is in ward to the Lord King together with his land in West Rasen; and he has been since the feast of Saint Martin[19] until now, and by order of the Lord King he is in the wardship of the sheriff, who through William fitz Siward took £19 4s 8½d from last year's farm, and £13 17s 10d from this year's.[20] The said land is worth £38 per annum and one mark, and 10 marks from the lady *de Merchez*, with the existing stock, viz. 6 plough-teams, 400 sheep, 30 cows, 2 bulls, 10 sows, 2 boars, and one farmhorse. And if the shortfall of 10 cows and 200 sheep were made good the said land would be worth £42 per annum. This land was ordered to be stocked. Peter Paynel's widow is in the Lord King's gift.

(*Marginal note*: to be stocked)

---

[16] Presumably Michaelmas 1184.

[17] The half-carrucate of land had been given to the Augustinian canons of Thornton by Adam de Montbegon, Roger's predecessor: Round, *RD*, 5–6, n. 4.

[18] For other instances of this notation see nos. 11, 15, 185, and 186.

[19] 11 November 1184.

[20] This would make a total of £33 2s 6½d, not £33 1s 10d, as in Round, *RD*, xxi. The sheriff accounted for £54 12s in the pipe roll for this year: *Pipe Roll 31 Henry II*, 93.

Schirebech Wapentak'

12. Comitissa de Richemunt, que est soror Regis Scotorum, habet in nundinis de Sancto Botulfo redditum .viij. *m.* vel ampliorem, scilicet, quando nundine sunt bone; et .j. culturam habet in campis, que valet .x. *s.*; de firma ville Sancti Botulfi habet annuatim .iiij. *l.*, quas Ricardus prepositus recepit per preceptum Reinerii. Comitissa fuit dissaisita [de] terra sua per preceptum Regis, et interim cepit Reinerius de terra sua in villa Sancti Botulfi .vj. *l.* et .ij. *s.*

13. Uxor Simonis de Crieuequeor, que fuit filia Roberti filii Ernisii de Gousel', est in donatione Domini Regis. Terra sua in Huddintun' valet .c. *s.* et est de feodo Walteri de Neuill'. Terra illa non potest plus valere. Ipsa est .xxiiij. annorum, et habet .ij. filios et ij. filias. Primogenitus est .v. annorum et est in custodia matris per Dominum Regem.

14. Aliz Basset est in donatione Domini Regis et habet .vj. bovatas terre in Bunetorp quas tenet in capite de Rege; et valent per annum .viij. *l.*

Skirbeck Wapentake[21]

12. The countess of Richmond, sister of the King of Scots, has rent of 8 marks from the Boston Fairs, or more when the fairs are thriving; and she has one furlong in the fields, which is worth 10s. She has £4 per annum from the farm of the vill of Boston, which Richard, the reeve, received by order of Reiner.[22] The countess was dispossessed of her land by order of the Lord King, and in the interim Reiner took £6 2s from her land in the vill of Boston.

(Yarborough Wapentake)

13. The widow of Simon de Crevequer, daughter of Robert fitz Ernis of Goxhill, is in the Lord King's gift. Her land in Honington is worth 100s and belongs to the fee of Walter de Neville. The land cannot be worth more. She is 24 years old and has two sons and two daughters. The firstborn son is five years old and through the Lord King is in his mother's wardship.[23]

(Calcewath Wapentake)

14. Alice Basset is in the Lord King's gift and has 6 bovates of land in Bonthorpe, which she holds in chief of the Lord King; and they are worth £8 per annum.[24]

---

[21] There had been a late twelfth-century re-naming of the Domesday wapentake of Wolmersty: P. Morgan and C. Thorn, eds., *Domesday Book, Lincolnshire* (Chichester, 1986), vol. 31, pt. 2, Index of Places (unpaginated).

[22] Rannulf Glanvill's steward. In 1183 Rannulf Glanvill accounted for 60s from the profits of the Boston Fair: *Pipe Roll 29 Henry II*, 58.

[23] See no. 37, where only the sons are recorded. Round, *RD*, 7, n. 2, comments on but does not resolve the problem that Simon de Crevequer appears to be alive at the time of the pipe roll for 1185: *Pipe Roll 31 Henry II*, 84. I. J. Sanders, *English Baronies* (Oxford, 1960), 74, simply has Simon's death as *ante* 1185. Entry no. 37 suggests that it was fairly recent.

[24] Round, *RD*, 7, n. 3, comments that a value of £8 implies a much larger holding. This Alice Basset, otherwise known as Alice of Dunstanville, was probably the widow of Thomas Basset and mother of Gilbert Basset.

15. Terra Alberti Gresle in Sexeleia cum pertinentiis valuit die qua obiit .iiij. *l.* et
.x. *s.* et hoc fuit instauramentum, .iiij. carruce quelibet .viij. boum, et .iij. boves,
.iij. vacce, .ii. juvence et .c. et .iiij.ˣˣ· et .xv. oves et .xxviij. porci. Thomas Basset
et Gilebertus, filius ejus, habuerunt custodiam per preceptum Domini Regis per
.j. annum. Thomas recepit inde .ij. firmas, scilicet, .xlj. *s.* et .vj. *d.* et .xl. summas
frumenti, et de brasio .xxx. summas, de avena .x. summas, quas omnes expendit
apud Linc' et in terra Alberti; et in adventu suo ad Sexeleiam expendit .x. summas de frumento et avenam que valuit .xlv. *s.* Gilebertus Basset recepit inde de
firma .xlj. *s.* et .vj. *d.* et de placitis .iij. *m.*; de blado .xij. *m.*; de lana .v. *m.* et dim.;
de .iij. bobus et .ij. juvencis .x. *s.* Istud manerium cum firma et instauramento et
perquisitionibus fuit affirmatum per preceptum Domini Regis per Gilebertum
Basset et Radulfum Gibewin pro .xx. *l.* per annum; et traditum Alic', pretori, et
Roberto de Heinton' et Willelmo filio Roberti et Willelmo filio Turoldi, qui
illud tenuerunt per .j. annum, et reddiderunt quartam partem firme, scilicet, .c.
s. Gileberto Basset, et .xv. *l.* ejusdem firme Nigello filio Alexandri et Roberto
de Burun. Et ex . . . . . .Nigellus filius Alexandri . . . . . .ⁱᵛ tenuerunt et tenent illud manerium per dictam firmam. Et preter dictum instauramentum possunt ibi
esse .xlv. oves, que si apponerentur, firma posset augeri de .xij. *s.* Et preceptum
est staurari.

Marginal note: Instaur'.

16. Filius Hereberti filii Gileberti est in custodia Domini Regis, et .x. annorum,
et terra sua de Rigesbi est de feodo archiepiscopatus Eboracensis, que fuit seisita
in manum Domini Regis per custodes archiepiscopatus ad festum Sancti Botulfi

---

ⁱᵛ Space left blank.

(Wraggoe Wapentake)

15. The land of Albert Grelley in Sixhills with its appurtenances was worth £4 10s (per annum) on the day that he died,[25] and this was the stock: 4 plough-teams, each of 8 oxen,[26] plus 3 oxen, 3 cows, 2 heifers, 195 sheep, and 28 pigs. Thomas Basset and Gilbert, his son, had wardship for one year by order of the Lord King. Thomas received two farms from there, viz. 41s 6d and 40 pack-loads of wheat, 30 pack-loads of malt, 10 pack-loads of oats, all of which he used at Lincoln and on Albert's land.[27] On his arrival at Sixhills he used 10 pack-loads of wheat and oats, which were worth 45s. Gilbert Basset received 41s 6d from the farm, 3 marks from pleas, 12 marks from grain, 5½ marks from wool, and 10s from (the sale of) 3 oxen and 2 heifers. This manor with its farm, stock, and perquisites was farmed out by order of the Lord King through Gilbert Basset and Ralph Gibewin for £20 per annum; and (it was) handed over to *Alic'*, the reeve, Robert de Heinton, William fitz Robert, and William fitz Turold. They held it for one year and rendered a quarter of the farm, namely 100s, to Gilbert Basset, and £15 of the same farm to Nigel fitz Alexander and Robert de Burun. And from . . . Nigel fitz Alexander . . . [and Robert de Burun?] . . . held and hold this manor by the said farm. And beside the said stock there could be 45 sheep, which, if placed there, could increase the farm by 12s. And it was ordered to be stocked.

(Marginal note: to be stocked)

(Calcewath Wapentake)

16. The son of Herbert fitz Gilbert is in ward to the Lord King and is ten years old. His land in Rigsby belongs to the fee of the archbishopric of York and was seized into the Lord King's hand by the archbishop's custodians at the feast of

---

[25] Albert Grelley died c. 1181: Round, *RD*, 4, n. 2. Thomas Basset died probably a year later: Reedy, *Basset Charters*, xiii.

[26] This is the first of eight such references to plough-teams of 8 oxen. The others are at nos. 40, 72, 106, 131, 132, 143, and 153. Three entries (nos. 122, 133, and 173) refer to mixed plough-teams of 6 oxen and 2 horses. Five entries (nos. 4, 76, 80, 163, and 179) refer to stock of 8 oxen or a multiple of 8 without specifically mentioning plough-teams. It seems reasonably clear from this that, as at the time of Domesday Book, 8-oxen plough-teams or the equivalent were still the norm. See S. Harvey, "Taxation and the Ploughland in Domesday Book," in P. Sawyer, ed., *Domesday Book: A Reassessment* (London, 1985), 86–103.

[27] The pack-load or cart-load was probably the London quarter of 8 bushels: R. E. Zupko, *British Weights and Measures* (Madison, 1977), 18–19.

proximo preteritum: et redditus dicte terre sunt .xxx. *s* . . . .[v]est ibi instaura-mentum, et si essent ibi .ij. carruce et .cc. oves et .xv. vacce et .iiij. sues et .j. verris, terra valeret .x. *l.* et .vij. *s.*

17. Uxor Roberti filii Hugonis est in donatione Domini Regis et est .l. annorum. Dos sua valet .xx. *l.* cum .iiij. carrucis et .cc. ovibus et .xv. vaccis; et non sunt ibi nisi .iij. carruce et .lx. oves et .vii. vacce. Ipsa fuit filia Willelmi filii Walteri de Welle et habet .x. pueros.

Marginal note: Hornecastr' wapentak'.

18. Filius Willelmi filii Chetelli, ostriciarii Domini Regis, est de custodia Domini Regis et in custodia matris sue per Dominum Rannulfum de Glanuill', et est .xij. annorum. Willelmus Basset, vicecomes, saisivit terram suam, et nihil inde cepit, quia mater heredis finivit statim cum Domino Rannulfo pro .x. *m.* de custodia filii sui . . .[vi] ut liceret ei nubere ad voluntatem suam. Et Willelmus filius Chetelli nihil tenuit in capite de Domino Rege, preter illud quod tenuit de Rege in soka de Hornecastro, et per firmam quam reddebat Gerebod' de Escaliis, qui tenuit socham de Hornecastro, et adhuc tenet per ann' . . .[vii]

[Rot. 1. d.]

19. Heres Willelmi de Vesci est .xiiij. annorum, et in custodia Domini Regis. Quando Adamus de Carduill recepit custodiam terre sue in Cattorp', invenit ibi .xxviij. boves, quorum unus mortuus fuit; et .v. averos, quorum unus mortuus

---

[v] Possibly "et .i. d.," but the whole sum is illegible even under ultra-violet treatment. Given the great difference between the actual value and the potential value, it is possible that "non" should precede "est ibi instauramentum."

[vi] MS damaged. Perhaps "et" should be understood.

[vii] MS damaged.

Saint Botolph last past.[28] The rents of the said land are 30s . . .[29] and there is (no?) stock there, and if there were 2 plough-teams, 200 sheep, 15 cows, 4 sows, and one boar the land would be worth £10 7s.[30]

(Horncastle Wapentake)

17. The widow of Robert fitz Hugh is in the Lord King's gift and she is 50 years of age. Her dower is worth £20 (per annum) with 4 plough-teams, 200 sheep, and 15 cows. There are only 3 plough-teams, 60 sheep, and 7 cows. She herself was the daughter of William fitz Walter of Wells and has ten sons.[31]

(*Marginal note*: Horncastle Wapentake)

18. The son of William fitz Chetel, the Lord King's goshawk keeper, is in ward to the Lord King and through Rannulf Glanvill is in the wardship of his mother, and he is 12 years old. William Basset, the sheriff, seized his land and took nothing from it, because the heir's mother immediately paid a fine of 10 marks to Lord Rannulf for the wardship of her son . . . (and?) so that it would be lawful for her to marry at her own will.[32] And William fitz Chetel held nothing in chief of the Lord King, except that which he held in the soke of Horncastle, and by reason of the farm which Gerbod de Eschaud used to render, who held the soke of Horncastle, and still holds per annum . . .[33]

[Roll 1. dorse.]

(Loveden Wapentake)

19. William de Vesci's heir is 14 years of age and in ward to the Lord King. When Adam of Carlisle received wardship of William's land in Caythorpe he found 28 oxen there, of which one was dead, five farm-horses, of which one was dead, 7

---

[28] 17 June 1184.

[29] The MS is virtually illegible here.

[30] See no. 20. The widow of Herbert fitz Gilbert had apparently remarried and was widowed again.

[31] See nos. 9 and 21. The marginal note probably relates back to entry no. 9. The location of the widow's dower is not mentioned.

[32] In the previous year Alice, William fitz Chetel's wife, had accounted for ten marks at the Exchequer, paying six and owing four: *Pipe Roll 30 Henry II*, 20.

[33] See *Pipe Roll 20 Henry II*, 96–97. The farm had been worth £40. For the continued existence of the soke as a territorial and judicial unit in the twelfth and thirteenth centuries see D. C. Douglas, *The Social Structure of Medieval East Anglia* (Oxford, 1927), chap. 4. Gerbod was probably one of Henry II's Flemish captains of mercenaries: Round, *RD*, 9, n. 2.

fuit; .vij. porcos unius anni, et .viij. minores; et .dc. oves, de quibus .cc. et .lx. fuerunt vendite .xv. *m*. et .xj. *s*. et .viij. *d*.; de residuis, mortue fuerunt .cc. et .iiij. ^{xx.} quarum pelles vendite fuerunt .iiij. *l*. et .xij. *s*. Idem cepit de firma per Reginaldum de Friston' primo anno .xxxix. *l*. et .ix. *s*. et .x. *d*. et .j. capellum de pavone de redditu Willelmi de Pinkennia. Postea recepit Hugo de Morewich' custodiam de Cattorp', et invenit ibi .xxvij. boves et .iiij. averias (*sic*) et .j. vitulum et .ij. sues et .vij. porcos juvenes et .l. oves et .xxxiij. pelles et .xvij. que nullius sunt precii. Cattorp' cum pertinentiis potest valere per annum .xxxvj. *l*. et .xvj. *s*. et. .v. *d*. si esset ibi rationabile instauramentum quod posset sustineri, scilicet, .v. carruce, .d. oves, .ij. vacce, .iii. sues, .j. verris. Assisus redditus in dicta villa sunt .xxj. *l*.; et pratum de Widdenesse appreciatur annuatim cum dominico, et cum predicto instauramento, et cum placitis et perquisitionibus, .x. *l*. et .v. *s*. Preterea est ibidem quidam redditus de blado qui valet .j. *m*.; et cum instauramento quod ibi est valet manerium .xxx. *l*. et .iiij. *s*. et .j. *d*. et *ob*. Dicta villa fuit in manu Domini Regis elapsis .ij. annis ante Pascha proximo preteritum, et dum fuit in manu Ade de Carduill', vicecomes cepit inde de auxilio .x. *s*. De matre dicti heredis nesciunt juratores an sit in donatione Domini Regis, quia nullum habet tenementum nisi dotem suam quam tenet de hereditate filii sui, cui facit inde servitium.

Kalsewath Wapentach

20. In Risebi, que est de feodo archiepiscopatus Eboracensis, est que[dam] vidua Galfridi de Turs et neptis Galfridi de Nouill', que fuit uxor Hereberti filii Gileberti; et est de donatione Domini Regis per archiepiscopatum, et est .xxx. annorum et habet .vij. pueros, quorum primogenitus est .x. annorum, et in custodia custodum archiepiscopatus. Ipsa nullam habet terram nisi dotem suam, que valet annuatim .lxij. *s*. cum instauramento unius carruce que ibi est; et si adderentur .lx. oves et dimidia carruca, terra valeret per annum .iiij. *l*. et .vj. *s*.

21. Elisabeth, que fuit uxor Roberti filii Hugonis, habet in Meltesbi .c. *s*. redditus de maritagio suo de feodo Willelmi filii Walteri.

yearling pigs, and 8 piglets, 600 sheep, of which 260 were sold for 15 marks and 11s 8d.[34] Of the remainder 280 were dead and their pelts sold for £4 12s. The same man (Adam) took £39 9s 10d in the first year from the farm, through Reginald of Friston, and rent of one headpiece of peacock's feathers from William de Pinkney. Afterwards Hugh de Morwich received wardship of Caythorpe and found there 27 oxen, 4 farm-horses, one calf, 2 sows, 7 young pigs, 50 sheep, 33 pelts, and 17 pelts which have no value. Caythorpe with its appurtenances could be worth £36 16s 5d, if sufficient amount of stock were maintained there, viz. 5 plough-teams, 500 sheep, 2 cows, 3 sows, and one boar. The fixed rents in the said vill amount to £21. The meadow of Widdenesse, with the demesne, and with the aforesaid stock, pleas, and perquisites, is worth £10 5s (per annum). Furthermore, there is a certain grain rent there worth one mark. And with the existing stock the manor is worth £30 4s 1½d. The said vill was in the Lord King's hand for two years before last Easter,[35] and while it was in Adam of Carlisle's hand the sheriff took 10s in aid from it. As for the mother of the said heir, the jurors do not know if she is in the Lord King's gift, because she has no holding except her dower, which she holds of the inheritance of her son, to whom she does service.

Calcewath Wapentake

20. In Rigsby, which belongs to the fee of the archbishop of York, there is a certain widow of Geoffrey de Turs and niece of Geoffrey *de Nouill'*, who was (also) the widow of Herbert fitz Gilbert, and she is in the Lord King's gift through the archbishopric. She is 30 years of age and has seven boys, of whom the eldest is 10, and he is in the wardship of the archbishop's custodians.[36] She herself has no land except her dower, which is worth 62s per annum with stock of one plough-team, which is there; and if 60 sheep and half a plough-team were added the land would be worth £4 6s per annum.

21. Elizabeth, widow of Robert fitz Hugh, has 100s in rent at Maltby as her marriage portion from the fee of William fitz Walter (her father).[37]

---

[34] I.e. approximately 10d per sheep. This seems extraordinarily high, but see D. Farmer, "Prices and Wages" in *Agrarian History of England and Wales*, 2: 715–817, and Table D, 800.

[35] Easter 1185.

[36] There was a vacancy at York in 1185. See nos. 5 and 16.

[37] See nos. 9 and 17.

22. Roeis de Bussei, que fuit filia Baldewini filii Gileberti et uxor Willelmi de Bussei, est in donatione Domini Regis, et est .l. annorum; et habet duas filias, quarum primogenitam habet Johannes de Builli, et alteram Hugo Wak' per Dominum Regem. Heritagium suum in Morton' valet .xv. *l.* per annum, cum instauramento .iij. carrucarum et .cc. ovium. Terra quam modo habet ibi valet .iiij. *l.*, et superplus habent .ij. filie sue, et alii homines qui tenent per servitium suum.

23. Agnes, que fuit uxor Walteri de Hacunbi et filia Colgrim de Weleburn', est de donatione Domini Regis, et est .xl. annorum, et habet .ij. filios et .ij. filias. Major natu filiorum est .xviij. annorum et in custodia matris per Dominum Regem pro .v. *m.* quas ipsa dedit Regi, et vicecomes eas recepit: et terra sua est de eschaeta Domini Regis de Hacunbi, et valet .iiij. *l.* per annum, nec potest plus valere.

24. Matillis de La Haia, que fuit filia Willelmi de Vernun et uxor Ricardi de La Haia, est de donatione Domini Regis, et est .lvij. annorum; et habet .iij. filias, quarum .j. habet Gerardus de Camuill', et alteram Ricardus de Humez, tertiam Willelmus de Rolles. Swauueton', que est dos ejus, valet .xxx. *l.* per annum, cum instauramento quod ibi est; scilicet, .iij. carrucis et .lx. ovibus, .x. suibus, et .j. verre; et si adderentur .lx. oves et .vj. vacce et .j. taurus, posset terra valere .xxx. *l.* et .xvi. *s.*

Aswarehirne Wapentak'

25. Filius Willelmi filii Rannulfi est in custodia Domini Regis per episcopatum et in custodia Hugonis Bardulf per Dominum Regem, et ipse est .viij. annorum. Hugo Bardulf recepit de terra sua in Iwarebi his .iij. annis .xv. *m.* quibus fuit in

(Aveland Wapentake)

22. Rose de Bussy, daughter of Baldwin fitz Gilbert (de Clare) and widow of William de Bussy, is in the Lord King's gift, and she is 50 years of age. She has two daughters, of whom the elder is married to John de Builli and the other to Hugh Wake with the Lord King's permission. Her inheritance in Morton is worth £15 per annum, with stock of 3 plough-teams and 200 sheep. The land she has there now is worth £4, and the remainder is held by her two daughters and other men who hold by virtue of their service.[38]

23. Agnes, widow of Walter of Haconby and daughter of Colgrim *de Weleburn'*, is in the Lord King's gift, is 40 and has two sons and two daughters. The elder son is 18 and is in his mother's wardship by order of the Lord King for 5 marks, which she paid to the King, and the sheriff has received payment. Her land belongs to the Lord King's escheat of Haconby and is worth £4 per annum and cannot be worth more.[39]

24. Matilda de la Haye, daughter of William de Vernon and widow of Richard de la Haye, is in the Lord King's gift. She is 57 and has three daughters, of whom one is married to Gerard de Camville, another to Richard du Hommet,[40] and the third to William de Rolles. Her dower of Swaton is worth £30 per annum with the existing stock, viz. 3 plough-teams, 60 sheep, 10 sows, and one boar; and if 60 sheep, 6 cows, and one bull were added the land would be worth £30 16s.

Aswardhurn Wapentake

25. The son of William fitz Rannulf is in ward to the Lord King on account of the bishopric,[41] and through the Lord King he is in the wardship of Hugh Bardulf.[42] He is 8 years of age. Hugh Bardulf received 15 marks from his land in Ewerby for

---

[38] This is the first of 16 extracts translated and edited by Amt, *Women's Lives in Medieval Europe*, 154–57. The other 15 entries — some of them incomplete — are nos. 36, 37, 46, 47, 49, 53, 56, 64, 68, 69, 72, 73, 80, 110, and 114. Rose de Bussy appears only as the daughter of Baldwin fitz Gilbert in no. 103, where she is recorded as 60 years of age.

[39] This escheat can be traced back at least as far as 1164 when the sheriff acounted for 59s 4d: *Pipe Roll 10 Henry II*, 23.

[40] Richard du Hommet was sheriff of Rutland for most of Henry II's reign and constable of Normandy 1154–1180. Gerard de Camville, who married Nicola de la Haye, was later constable of Lincoln Castle and sheriff of Lincolnshire and was a staunch supporter of King John: Poole, *Domesday Book to Magna Carta*, 355, 366, and 485. See also Johns, *Noblewomen*, 160–61.

[41] There was a vacancy at Lincoln in 1185.

[42] Hugh Bardulf was a younger son of the baronial family and began his judicial career in 1184: M. S. Walker, ed., *Feet of Fines for the County of Lincoln for the Reign of King John 1199–1216*, Pipe Roll Society Publications 67, n.s. 29 (Lincoln, 1953), xxxii.

manu ejus. Terra illa valet annuatim. .v. *m*. et non potest plus valere quia nullum potest ibi esse instauramentum.

26. Robertus, filius Osberti Seluein, est in custodia Domini Regis per episcopatum Lincolniensem a festo Sancte Crucis in Augusto, et est .xj. annorum et dim. Terra sua in Wilebi, cum .iij. carrucis que ibi sunt in dominio, et .ij. *m*. que ibi sunt de firma, valet per annum .vij. *l*. et vij. *s*. et viij. *d*. Et si ibi essent .cc. oves, valeret terra annuatim .xj. *l*. et dim. *m*. Jocelinus de Euermuwa recepit dictam firmam postquam fuit in manu Domini Regis, et .j. libram piperis et .j. libram cumini et .ij. *d*. Ricardus Brit' et Robertus de Hardres duxerunt inde ad castellum de La Forde .c. et .xj. esceppas bladi, quod valuit .ix. *l*. et .xviij. *s*.

Flaxwelle Wapentak'

27. Uxor que fuit Roberti de Cauz et mater uxoris Radulfi filii Stephani, camberlani Domini Regis, filia Ricardi Basset et soror Willelmi Basset, est de donatione Domini Regis, et est .1. annorum et amplius. Terra ejus in Riscint', cum pertinentiis, valet .xij. *l*. per annum, cum instauramento quod ibi est; scilicet, ij. carrucis, .c. ovibus, .v. vaccis, .j. tauro; et si adderentur .c. oves que desunt, valeret per annum .xiiij. *l*. Hec terra est de baronia Radulfi filii Stephani.

28. Uxor Alberti Gresle fuit de donatione Domini Regis, et in ejus custodia per .j. annum et .iiij. partes anni, sub custodia Thome Basset; et intra hunc terminum reddiderunt, scilicet, Ricardus filius Siward' et Willelmus le Cornur domine sue de terra sua de Blacchesham .ix. *l*. et .iiij. *s*. et viij. *d*. de firma; et de blado vendito .c. *s*. et .xij. *d*. Dominus Rex dedit eam postea Widoni de Croun, cum terra sua in Blocchesham. Ipsa habet .j. filium heredem terre sue qui est in custodia Domini Regis; et est .xj. annorum. Et tota baronia est in custodia Nigel filii Alexandri per preceptum Domini Regis.

the three years that it was in his possession. The land is worth 5 marks per annum and cannot be worth more because no stock can be sustained there.

26. Robert, son of Osbert Selvein, is in ward to the Lord King on account of the bishopric of Lincoln since the feast of the Holy Cross in August and he is 11½ years of age.[43] His land in Willoughby, together with 3 plough-teams, which are there in demesne, and two marks, which are of the farm, is worth £7 7s 8d per annum. And if there were 200 sheep the land would be worth £11 and half a mark per annum. Jocelin d'Envermeu received the said farm after it came into the Lord King's hand, together with one pound of pepper, one pound of cumin, and 2d. Richard Brito and Robert de Hardres took 111 baskets of grain, which were worth £9 18s, from there to Sleaford Castle. [44]

Flaxwell Wapentake

27. The widow of Robert de Caux, mother-in-law of Ralph fitz Stephen, the royal chamberlain, daughter of Richard Basset and sister of William Basset, is in the Lord King's gift and is more than 50 years of age. Her land in Ruskington, with its appurtenances, is worth £12 per annum, with the existing stock, viz. 2 plough-teams, 100 sheep, 5 cows, and one bull. And if the shortfall of 100 sheep were made good it would be worth £14.[45] This land belongs to the barony of Ralph fitz Stephen.

28. Albert Grelley's widow was in the Lord King's gift and in his wardship for one and three-quarter years in the custody of Thomas Basset; and in this period Richard fitz Siward and William le Cornur rendered to their lady from her land in Bloxholm £9 3s 8d from the farm (of the manor), and 101s from the sale of grain. Subsequently the Lord King gave her (in marriage) to Guy de Craon, together with her land in Bloxholm.[46] She herself has one son and heir, who is in ward to the Lord King, and he is 11 years old. And the whole barony is in the wardship of Nigel fitz Alexander by order of the Lord King.

---

[43] The pipe roll evidence confirms that Osbert fitz Selvein was alive in 1184 and deceased in 1185: *Pipe Roll 30 Henry II*, 15 and *Pipe Roll 31 Henry II*, 92. The feast of the Holy Cross is 14 September.

[44] Sleaford Castle belonged to the bishops of Lincoln.

[45] Round, *RD*, 14, n. 1, suggests that this vill may well have been Rowston rather than Ruskington in Flaxwell Wapentake.

[46] Bloxholm was presumably her dower and went with her to Guy de Craon, who paid 200 marks to the Exchequer: *Pipe Roll 28 Henry II*, 57.

Balteslawe Wapentak'

29. Matillis de Diua, que fuit uxor Willelmi de Diua et filia Walteri de Gaufreuill', est de donatione Domini Regis, et est .xxxv. annorum. Terra sua de Corebi est de episcopatu Lincolniensi, et est maritagium suum et valet .vij. *m.* cum instauramento quod ibi est; scilicet, .j. carruca et .cxl. ovibus. Et si esset ibi alia carruca, et .iiij.ˣˣ oves, .vj. vacce et .j. taurus, .vj. sues et .j. verris, dicta villa posset valere per annum .x. *m.* et .v. *s.* et .iiij. *d.* Dicta domina habet .ij. filios et .ij. filias, et heres est .x. annorum et in custodia Willelmi de Diua.

30. Matillis Comitissa Cestrie est de donatione Domini Regis, et fuit filia Roberti Comitis Gloecestrie, filii Regis Henrici Primi, et est .l. annorum et amplius. Ipsa tenet Wadint' in dote de feodo comitis Cestrie, et firma sunt (*sic*) .xxij. *l.* per annum. Dicta villa valet per annum .xl. *l.* cum hoc instauramento, scilicet, .ij. carrucis, .iiij. vaccis, .j. tauro, .iiij. suibus, .j. verre, .d. ovibus que ibi sunt inter oves et multones et agnos; et non potest plus instauramenti pati. Redditus hujus ville recepit comitissa his .viij. annis.

Jeretre Wapentak'

31. Bertreia Comitissa, filia comitis de Everews, uxor Hugonis Comitis Cestrie, est de donatione Domini Regis, et est .xxix. annorum. Maritagium et dos ejus sunt ultra mare, et ideo nesciunt juratores quid valeant. Sed Dominus Rex precepit quod ipsa haberet .xl. libratas terre domini sui in Beltesford' et Hemmingebi et Duninton': sed non habuit nisi .xxxv. libratas et .x. solidatas, quia, ut dicunt, dicta terra non potest plus valere cum instauramento quod comitissa ibi recepit, scilicet, .v. carrucis et .ccc. et .xlj. ovibus et .x. suibus et .j. verre; sed si in

Beltisloe Wapentake

29. Matilda de Dives, widow of William de Dives and daughter of Walter of Waterville, is in the Lord King's gift and is 35 years of age. Her land of Corby belongs to the bishopric of Lincoln. It is her marriage portion and is worth 7 marks with the existing stock, viz. one plough-team and 140 sheep. And if another plough-team were there, together with 80 sheep, 6 cows, one bull, 6 sows, and one boar, the said vill would be worth 10 marks and 5s 4d per annum. The above widow has two sons and two daughters. The heir is 10 years old and in the wardship of William de Dives.[47]

(Boothby Wapentake)

30. Matilda, countess of Chester, is in the Lord King's gift. She was a daughter of Robert, earl of Gloucester, son of King Henry I, and she is more than 50 years old.[48] She herself holds Waddington in dower of the fee of the earl of Chester and the farm is £22 per annum. The said vill is worth £40 with the following stock: viz. 2 plough-teams, 4 cows, one bull, 4 sows, one boar, and 500 sheep, which as sheep, wethers, and lambs are there. And it is not possible to sustain more stock. The countess has received the rents of this vill for these (past) eight years.[49]

Gartree Wapentake

31. Countess Bertrada, daughter of the count of Evreux and widow of Hugh, earl of Chester,[50] is in the Lord King's gift and is 29. Her marriage portion and dower lie overseas, and so the jurors do not know how much they are worth. But the Lord King ordered that she should have 40 librates of her husband's land in Belchford, Hemingby, and Donington, but she had only 35 librates and 10 solidates,[51] because, according to the jurors, the said land cannot be worth more, given the stock the countess received there, namely 5 plough-teams, 341 sheep,

---

[47] The document does not reveal the identity of this William de Dives, as distinct from the deceased husband of the same name. See also no. 55, which gives the ages of all the children, including the heir, but as 12, rather than 10.

[48] Matilda, widow of Earl Rannulf of Chester (d. 16 December 1153).

[49] The first of ten references to an 8-year period, presumably since the previous enquiry, which would have been in 1177, the year after the Assize of Northampton. The other references are in nos. 46, 60, 76, 103, 139, 145, 162–163, and 167.

[50] Earl Hugh of Chester, d. 30 June 1181.

[51] In other words, land worth £35 10s rather than £40, which is confirmed in the final valuation if the land were fully stocked.

Duninton' apponerentur .cc. oves et .x. sues et .j. verris, tunc valeret terra quam comitissa habet, .xl. *l.*

Jareburg Wapentak

32. In Staliburg' habet Thomas de Areci .ij. carrucatas terre et .ij. bovatas, quas tenet in baronia de Domino Rege; et valent per annum .xvj. *l.* et xv. *s.* cum instauramento .ij. carrucarum que ibi sunt; et si ibi essent .iiij. carruce et .xx. vacce et .ij. tauri et .x. sues et .ij. verres et .m. et .c. oves, dicta terra valeret per annum .xl. *l.* Ipsa fuit in manu Domini Regis elapsis .ij. annis a festo Sancti Mathei proximo preterito. Michael de Arceia et Hereueus de Horsint', qui fuerunt cus-todes, receperunt de firma .x. *m..* et .xij. *d.*, et de prato vendito .ij. annorum, .viij. *m.* et .ix. *s.* et .iiij. *d.* Dictus Thomas est .xviij. annorum et habet .ij. fratres juniores se, et .iiij. sorores, quarum .j. fuit maritata vivente patre S'^{viii} de Muntbegun; et .ij. sunt nubiles; tertia (*sic*) est .viij. annorum; et sunt nati de baronibus. Dictus Thomas tenet de Domino Rege feoda .xx. militum; et de feodo Willelmi de Perci feoda .v. militum.

33. Avicia de Crieuequor est de donatione Domini Regis, et est .lxx. annorum. Ipsa habet feodum .j. militis in dominio de feodo comitis Legrecestr'; et de illo feodo habet in Croxt' .iij. carrucatas terre, que valent per annum .xiiij. *l.*, cum instauramento .c. ovium et .ij. carrucarum que ibi sunt: nec potest plus valere, nec plus instauramenti pati. Robertus de Bouesboz, filius filii sui, est heres ejus, et est .xxij. annorum; habet etiam .iiij. filias, quas Dominus Rex maritavit.

Braitele Wapentak'

34. Mater Radulfi de Humestain, que est consanguinea Radulfi filii Drogonis, est de donatione Domini Regis, et est plusquam .lx. annorum. Ipsa habet .ij. bovatas terre in dote, que ei reddunt annuatim dim. *m.* Ipsa habet .ij. filios: unum .xxx. annorum, alium .xxiiij. annorum, et .j. filiam .xx. annorum.

---

^{viii} According to Round, *RD*, 16, n. 2, this is a doubtful letter written over an erasure. The MS appears to have been damaged by water.

10 sows, and one boar; but if 200 sheep, 10 sows, and one boar were added to Donington, then the countess's land would be worth £40.

Yarborough Wapentake

32. Thomas Darcy has two carrucates and two bovates of land in Stallingborough, which he holds in barony of the Lord King; and they are worth £16 15s per annum with stock of two plough-teams, which are there. But if there were 3 plough-teams, 20 cows, 2 bulls, 10 sows, 2 boars, and 1,100 sheep the land would be worth £40 per annum. The land was in the Lord King's hand for two years as of the feast of St Matthew last past.[52] Michael Darcy and Hervey of Horsington, the custodians, received 10 marks and 12d from the farm (of the manor) and 8 marks, 9s 3d from the sale of meadow for two years. The above Thomas is 18 and has two younger brothers and four sisters, of whom one was married while her father was alive to S.[53] of Montbegon; and two are unmarried, and the third (*sic*) is 8 years of age, and they were born of barons. The said Thomas holds 20 knights' fees of the Lord King, and 5 knights' fees of the fee of William de Percy.[54]

33. Avice de Crevequer is in the Lord King's gift and is 70 years old. She holds one knight's fee in demesne belonging to the fee of the earl of Leicester; and of that fee she holds 3 carrucates of land in Croxton, which are worth £14 per annum with stock of 100 sheep and two plough-teams, which are there, nor can it be worth more, or sustain more stock. Robert de Bonesboz, her grandson, is her heir and he is 22 years old. She also has three daughters whom the Lord King has given in marriage.

Bradley Wapentake

34. The mother of Ralph of Humberston, who is a kinswoman of Ralph fitz Drogo, is in the Lord King's gift and is more than 60 years old. She has two bovates of land in dower, which return half a mark per annum to her. She has two sons, one 30, the other 24, and one daughter who is 20.

---

[52] 21 September 1184.
[53] Round, *RD*, 16, n. 2, indicates that this is a doubtful letter written over an erasure.
[54] See no. 4.

Haiwardho Wapentak'

35. Helewis de Swinope est de donatione Domini Regis, et est .l. annorum et amplius; et est Flandrensis natione, et fuit uxor Simonis de Canti (*sic*). Terra sua valet annuatim .x. *l.*, cum instauramento quod ibi est, scilicet, .ij. carrucis, .v. vaccis, .c. et .lx. ovibus et .viij. porcis; nec potest plus instauramenti pati, nec terra plus valere. De dictis .x. *l.* reddit ipsa annuatim .v. *m.* filio suo Simoni. Medietas feodi pertinet ad Dominum Regem. Alia medietas ad comitem Britannie.

36. Uxor Walteri Furmage, que fuit filia Thome de Neuill', est in donatione Domini Regis, et est .xxiiij. annorum, et habet filiam heredem, qua nondum est unius anni. Ipsa habet dimidiam carrucatam terre in Crosholm, pro qua reddit annuatim .v. *s.*, et potest poni ad firmam cum molendino pro .ij. *m.* Eadem habet in Sinterbi (*sic*) .iiij. bovatas terre, quas habet in dominio, et arat eas cum una carruca, et sunt maritagium suum de feodo patris sui, et valet terra per annum .xij. *s.*

37. Uxor Simonis de Crieuequor, que fuit filia Roberti filii Ernisii et filia filie Johannis Ingelram, est de donatione Domini Regis, et est .xxiiij. annorum; et habet .ij. filios: major natu est .v. annorum, minor vero .iiij. Terra sua in Hanewurth' valet annuatim .c. *s.* et non potest plus valere. Post mortem Simonis de Crieuequor terra de Hakent' fuit in manu Domini Regis, et preceptum fuit vicecomiti, quod uxor Simonis cum filiis suis inde haberet necessaria: et vicecomes per preceptum Domini Regis dimidio anno invenit ei necessaria, et vix potuit dimidio anno de manerio ei necessaria invenire. Haketorn', cum instauramento .ij. carrucarum, quas uxor Simonis post mortem ejus invenit, valet per annum .c. *s.* et .x: *s.*: .ij. carruce valent per annum .lx. *s.* et redditus assisi cum operationibus, .l. *s.*; et si essent ibi .cc. oves et .ij. vacce et .ij. sues, terra valeret .viij. *l.* et .x. *s.* Vicecomes nichil inde recepit, nisi quod expendit in inveniendo predicte domine necessaria, et quod in hoc expendit valuit .c. *s.*

At the foot of the roll: Tercii Buch' Linc' scirarum de custodiis et e . . . .

Haverstoe Wapentake

35. Helewis of Swinhope is in the Lord King's gift and is more than 50 years old; she is Flemish and was Simon de Canci's wife. Her land is worth £10 per annum with the existing stock, viz. 2 plough-teams, 5 cows, 160 sheep, and 8 pigs. Nor can it sustain more stock or the land be worth more. From the £10 she renders 5 marks annually to her son, Simon. Half of the fee belongs to the Lord King, the other half to the count of Brittany.

(Aslacoe Wapentake)

36. The widow of Walter Furmage, daughter of Thomas de Neville, is in the Lord King's gift and is 24 years of age. She has a daughter as heir, who is not yet one year old. She has half a carrucate of land in Crosholm, for which she renders 5s per annum, and it can be put at farm with the mill for 2 marks. In Snitterby she has 4 bovates, which she holds in demesne, and she cultivates them with one plough-team, and they are her marriage portion from her father's fee, and the land is worth 12s per annum.

37. The widow of Simon de Crevequer, daughter of Robert fitz Ernis and grand-daughter of John Ingelram,[55] is in the Lord King's gift and is 24 years of age. She has two sons: the elder is 5 years of age, the younger is 4. Her land in Hanworth is worth 100s per annum, and cannot be worth more.[56] After Simon de Crevequer's death the land of Hackthorn was in the Lord King's hand and the sheriff was instructed that Simon's widow together with her sons should receive their essential needs from there; and the sheriff, on the Lord King's order, provided subsistence for half a year and he was scarcely able to do so from the manor for that half year. Hackthorn with its stock of two plough-teams, which Simon's widow acquired on her husband's death, is worth 110s: two plough-teams worth 60s per annum and fixed rents with labour services worth 50s. And if there were 200 sheep, two cows, and two sows the land would be worth £8 10s. The sheriff received nothing from there, except his expenses in providing necessities for the said widow, and what he spent on this amounted to 100s.

At the foot of the roll: Concerning wardships of the shires of Buckingham (?) and Lincoln . . .

---

[55] This is the only direct reference to an heiress's grandfather; there is a more indirect reference in no. 63. There is also a reference to an heir's grandfather in no. 43. Cf. van Houts, *Memory and Gender in Medieval Europe*, 82.

[56] See no. 13.

[Rot. 2.]

De dominabus pueris et puellis

38. Oliverus, filius Johannis de Eincurt, est .xxiiij. annorum, et est nepos Radulfi Murdac, et cum eo per Dominum Regem. Johannes de Eincurt obiit elapsis .ij. annis ad festum Sancti Leonardi; et tunc saisivit Willelmus Basset terram predicti Johannis de Langho in manum Domini Regis, sed nihil inde recepit. Postea commendata fuit terra illa Galfrido filio Pagani et Helie de Fenecurt, et ipsi inde receperunt .viij. *s.* Postea commendavit Dominus Rex dictam terram et Oliverum heredem Johannis Radulfo Murdac, qui eam tenuit .ij. annis et dimidio; qui primo anno recepit de Branston' .xv. *l.* et xij. *s.* et .vj. *d.* de redditu assiso; et secundo anno, .xx. *l.* de redditu assiso, de perquisitionibus .lx. *s.*, .iij. *d.* minus; de venditione bladi .c. *s.* De dimidio anno sequenti, recepit .ix. *l.* et .x. *s.* Quando Johannes obiit reddidit Bra[n]ston' .xv. *l.* de firma assisa; et modo reddit .xix. *l.* Monachi de Chirkested' habent dominium in vadimonio, et totam pasturam ejusdem ville, qui ita oneraverunt eam ovibus et aliis averiis, quod non potest plus sustinere. De Blangenia cepit Radulfus Murdac primo anno .x. *l.;* et .xviij. *s.* de firma assisa; de purcatto .j. *m.* Secundo anno cepit de firma .xvj. *l.* et .v. *s.* Dimidio anno sequenti, .iiij. *l.* et .x. *s.* Domina Aliz, uxor Johannis de Eincurt, cepit .c. *s.* de dote sua in predicta villa dimidio anno. Blangenia tempore Johannis valuit .xv. *l.* per annum, cum instauramento .j.^us carruce; et modo valet .xviij. *l.,* cum instauramento .iij. carrucarum, que ibi sunt, et cum .j. vacca et .j. vitulo et .j. equo; et non potest dicta villa plus instauramenti pati, propter averia monachorum de Kirchested', et fratrum de Simplingham, et fratrum Templi. Preterea Radulfus Murdac cepit .x. *l.* et .xij. *s.* et .j. *d.* in dicta villa de releviis et de terris que fuerunt in manu sua antequam homines finem fecissent. Post mortem Johannis de Eincurt, obiit Philippus, persona de Timberlanda, et canonici de Turgarton' tenent ecclesiam illam. Dictus Philippus solebat reddere dictis canonicis dim. *m.* nomine pensionis, sed nescitur ex cujus donatione dictus Philippus habuit dictam ecclesiam, sed pater ejus habuit illam ex donatione Walteri de Eincurt'.

[Roll 2.]

Concerning ladies, boys and girls

(Langoe Wapentake)

38. Oliver, son of John d'Eincourt, who is 24 years of age, is a nephew of Ralph Murdac and is with him by order of the Lord King. John d'Eincourt died two years ago on the feast of St. Leonard;[57] subsequently William Basset seized the land of the said John de Langoe into the Lord King's hand, but he received nothing from it. Afterwards the land was commended to Geoffrey fitz Payn and Elias de Fenecurt and they received 8s from it. Then the Lord King commended the land and Oliver, John's heir, to Ralph Murdac, who held it for two and a half years. In the first year he received £15 12s 6d from the fixed rent of Branston; and in the second year £20 from fixed rent, 59s 9d from perquisites (of court), and 100s from the sale of grain. In the following half-year he received £9 10s. At the time of John's death Branston returned £15 from the fixed farm, and now it renders £19. The monks of Kirkstead hold the demesne in pledge (mortgage), together with all the pasture of the same vill; and they have so burdened it with sheep and other livestock that it is unable to sustain more. In the first year Ralph Murdac took £10 18s from the fixed farm of Blankney, and one mark from purchases. In the second year he took £16 5s from the farm. In the following half-year £4 10s. Lady Alice, John d'Eincourt's widow, received 100s from her dower in the said vill in the half-year. Blankney was worth £15 in John d'Eincourt's time, with stock of one plough-team, and now it is worth £18 with stock of 3 plough-teams, which are there, together with one cow, one calf, and one horse; and the said vill is unable to support more stock on account of the livestock belonging to the monks of Kirkstead, the brothers of Sempringham, and the brothers of the Temple. Moreover, Ralph Murdac took £10 12s 1d from the said vill in reliefs and from lands that were in his hand before the men had paid their fines. After John d'Eincourt's death Philip, the parson of Timberland, died, and the canons of Thurgarton hold that church. The said Philip was accustomed to render half a mark by way of pension to the said canons, but it is not known by whose gift Philip held the said church, but his father held it of the gift of Walter d'Eincourt.[58]

---

[57] 6 November 1182. Sanders, *English Baronies*, 15, has 1183, but, since John must have died at least 2½ years before the *Rotuli*, 1182 is more likely. According to the cartulary of Thurgarton Priory, John and Alice d'Eincourt had four sons and two daughters: T. Foulds, ed., *The Thurgarton Cartulary* (Stamford, 1994), lxxi–lxxiii.

[58] This entry is discussed in Lally, "Secular Patronage," 164, where it is pointed out that the estate improved in value under Ralph Murdac.

39. Aliz de Eincurt, que fuit uxor Johannis de Eincurt, est in donatione Domini Regis, et habet .x. libratas terre in dote in Blangenia.

Nesse Wapentak'

40. Filius Petri de Cote est .xviij. annorum et in custodia abbatis de Wellebech, cum terra sua de Carlebi, que valet annuatim .iiij. *m.* et .xl. *d.* sine instauramento; et si apponeretur ibi .j. carruca de .viij. bobus, et .lx. oves et .ij. vacce, valeret dicta terra .vij. *m.* et .viij. *s.* et .viij. *d.*; et terra[ix] illa est de feodo episcopatus Lincolniensis. Et dictus Petrus occisus fuit elapsis .ij. annis ad festum Sancti Michaelis, et exinde recepit dictus abbas redditus de Carlebi.

Manlet Wapentach'

41. Matillis, que fuit uxor Reginaldi de Crieuequeor, est de donatione Domini Regis, et est .lx. annorum et amplius. In terra sua de Redburn' sunt .v. *m.* assise[x] in terris et molendinis, et potest dominium coli .ij. carrucis et dim; et fuerunt ibi .iiij. carruce, quas fecit amovere vicecomes per servientes suos. Et si in predicta terra essent .xx. vacce et .d. oves et .xx. porci, ipsa valeret annuatim .xv. *l.*

[Rot. 2. d.]

42. Berton', que fuit Willelmi Painel', est in custodia Domini Regis cum herede, qui est .iiij. annorum, et in custodia Willelmi Vavassoris per Dominum Regem. Tempore Willelmi Painel', qui fuit dominus ante Fulconem Painel', fuit Berton' posita ad firmam cum .ij. carrucis pro .xj. *l.*; et modo potest valere per annum .xj. *l.*, cum hoc instauramento; scilicet, .xviij. bobus, .xiij. vaccis et .j. tauro et .ij. stircis .ij. annorum et .ij. juvencis .ij. annorum et .ij. vitulis .j. anni et .v. vitulis presentis et .ij. hercioris et .ij. suibus et .iiij. porcis junioribus. Et hoc instauramentum totum ibi est, et non potest plus sustinere. Willelmus Vavassor recepit inde custodiam ad Pentecosten proximo preteritum. Et cepit inde .lx. *s.* de firma. Willelmus Basset habuit custodiam inde anno preterito et cepit inde de firma .xxii.*l.* et vj.

[ix] Corrected in MS from "villa."

[x] "redditus" seems to be understood.

39. Alice d'Eincourt, the widow of John d'Eincourt, is in the Lord King's gift and has 10 librates of dower land in Blankney.

Ness Wapentake

40. The son of Peter de Cotes is 18 years of age and is in ward to the abbot of Welbeck together with his land of Carlby, which is worth 4 marks and 40d, not counting stock. If one plough-team of 8 oxen were placed there, along with 60 sheep and two cows, the said land would be worth 7 marks and 8s 8d. And that land belongs to the fee of the bishopric of Lincoln. The said Peter died two years ago at Michaelmas and since then the above abbot has received the rents of Carlby.

Manley Wapentake

41. Matilda, the widow of Reginald de Crevequer, is in the Lord King's gift and is more than 60 years old. On her estate at Redbourne there are 5 marks of fixed rents from lands and mills, and the demesne can be cultivated with two and a half plough-teams; and there were 3 plough-teams there, which the sheriff made his serjeants remove. And if there were 20 cows, 500 sheep, and 20 pigs on the aforesaid land it would be worth £15.[59]

42. Broughton,[60] which belonged to William Paynel, is in the Lord King's wardship with the heir, who is three years of age, and he is in the wardship of William Vavassor[61] by order of the Lord King. In the time of William Paynel, who was the lord before Fulk Paynel, Broughton was farmed out with two plough-teams for £11; and now it can be worth £11 per annum with the following stock: viz. 18 oxen, 13 cows, one bull, 2 two-year-old bullocks, 2 two-year-old heifers, 2 yearling calves, 5 new calves, 2 harrowing beasts, 2 sows, and 4 younger pigs. And the whole of this stock is there and no more can be sustained. William Vavassor received wardship there at Pentecost last past, and took 60s from the farm. William Basset had wardship there the previous year and took £22 6s from the farm (of

---

[59] Round, *RD*, xxxv, indicates that there were two sons from this marriage: Alexander and Simon. Simon's widow is the subject of nos. 13 and 37.

[60] The identification of Broughton rather than Burton-upon-Stather is convincingly argued by Round, as are the date limits of the *Rotuli* to Whitsuntide to Michaelmas 1185: Round, *RD*, 21, n. 1. The concordance, however, between William Basset's farm in this roll and the pipe roll of 1184 is not as perfect as Round suggests: the two sums are £22 6s and £22 10s, respectively: *Pipe Roll 30 Henry II*, 21.

[61] One of the four justices for this circuit.

s., et de blado vendito .ij. *m.*, et de porcis venditis .ij. *s.*; et de firma presentis anni .lxxj. *s.* et .vij. *d.*, qui deberent dari ad festum Sancti Michaelis proximo venturum. Idem cepit de hominibus pro consilio et auxilio dim. *m.* Willelmus de Sapercot' cepit de Osberto serviente de blado vendito .xj. *s.* et .iiij. *d.* ad opus vicecomitis. Et fuit terra in manu Domini Regis elapso .j. anno ad festum Sancti Johannis Babtiste (*sic*) proximo preteritum.

[Rot. 3.]

De dominabus et pueris et puellis in Norhamton'sire

43. Robertus, filius Hugonis, qui est .xx. annorum, est in custodia Domini Regis cum terra sua. Ipse habet ex donatione quam fecit Dominus Rex Roberto filio Sewini, avo suo, in campis de Norhamt' .ij. carrucatas terre, quarum unam tenet Engelramus filius Henrici de dicto Roberto pro .ij. *s.* per annum, et ipse Robertus tenet aliam in manu sua, que valet per annum .xxiiij. *s.* et .viij. *d.*, cum hoc in-stauramento, scilicet, .iiij. bobus et .ij. tauris et .xvj. ovibus; iste .ij. carrucate terre valebant antiquitus .lx. *s.*, cum .xij. bobus et .c. ovibus, et .ij. averis. De redditu asiso habet extra portam orientalem .xviij. *s.*; extra portam de Nort .vj. *s.* de red-ditu asiso, et .vj. *d.*; et in Swinewelle Strete .xij. *s.* Unde Hospitale de Jerusalem tenet .ij. *s.*, de dono Roberti filii Sewini; infirmi Sancti Leonardi .vj. *s.*; canonici de Dunstaple .xij. *d.*; et Durandus .ij. *s.* pro servitio suo; et ipse Robertus tenet .xij. *d.* in manu sua. Tali modo reddebat terra predicta .iiij. *l.* et xvj. *s.* et vj. *d.* Et cum predicto instauramento et .iiij. vaccis, posset terra valere .c. *s.* Et preterea, idem Robertus tenet quoddam pratum de predicto dono Regis, quod jacet ad firmam de Norhamt', pro .xx. *s.*, et computantur ad Scheccarium Domino Regi, et dicitur Chingeshale. Et preter predictos redditus habet infra burgum et extra

the manor), 2 marks from the sale of grain, 2s from the sale of pigs, and 71s 7d from the farm of the current year, which ought to be rendered at the coming feast of Michaelmas. The same man took half a mark from the men for counsel and aid. William of Sapcote took from Osbert, the serjeant, 11s 3d from grain sold in the interest of the sheriff's work.[62] And the land was in the Lord King's hand for one year up to the feast last past of Saint John the Baptist.[63]

[Roll 3.]

Concerning ladies, boys, and girls in Northamptonshire

(Spelhoe Hundred)

43. Robert fitz Hugh, who is 20, is in ward to the Lord King, together with his land. As a result of a gift which the Lord King made to Robert fitz Sewin, his grandfather,[64] he has 2 carrucates of land in the fields of Northampton, of which one is held by Engelram, son of the said Robert,[65] for 2s per annum, and Robert himself holds the other in his own hand, which is worth 24s 8d per annum with the following stock: viz. 3 oxen, 2 bulls, and 16 sheep. In ancient times these two carrucates of land were worth 60s with 12 oxen, 100 sheep, and 2 farm-horses. From fixed rent he has 18s from outside the east gate, 6s 6d from outside the north gate, and 12s in Swinewelle Street. The Hospital of Jerusalem has 2s of the gift of Robert fitz Sewin; the infirm of Saint Leonard's 6s, the canons of Dunstable 12d, and Durand 2s for his service, and Robert himself retains 12d in his own hand. In this way the above land was accustomed to return £4 16s 6d.[66] And with the above stock and 4 cows the land could be worth 100s. Moreover, the same Robert holds a certain meadow for 20s as part of the above gift of the Lord King, which belongs to the farm of Northampton; and it is accounted for at the King's Exchequer, and is called Chingeshale.[67] And besides the above rents he has within

---

[62] Reedy, *Basset Charters*, xii, where it is suggested that this William of Sapcote was probably not William Basset.

[63] 29 August 1184.

[64] One of the very few references to a grandfather; here of a male heir. He was sheriff of Northampton 1170–1174. For the career of Robert fitz Sewin see Amt, *The Accession of Henry II*, 99–100.

[65] Therefore presumably Robert fitz Hugh's uncle.

[66] This is a correct total: 60s followed by the urban rents, which amounted to £1 16s 6d.

[67] This sum was regularly accounted for in the pipe rolls of the 1180s.

.vij. *l.* de redditu asiso, et .ij. *s.* et .iiij. *d.*, quos ipse tenet a pluribus annis, sine terra quam ipse tenet in Upton' de Domino Rege.

44. Emma, que fuit uxor Hugonis filii Roberti, et prius uxor Roberti de Sancto Paulo, et filia Henrici Tiart, est de donatione Domini Regis, et est .xl. annorum. Ipsa habet dotem in Oxeneford'sire, ex donatione Roberti de Sancto Paulo, que valet .l. *s.*; et de maritagio in Brint' .lxiij. *s.*, cum instauramento .ij. carrucarum, .c. ovium et .iiij. suum; et preterea habet in Norhamt' in dote, .j. domum ex dono Roberti de Sancto Paulo, que valet annuatim .viij. *l.* Et Dominus Rex dedit predictam feminam Hugoni filio Roberti, cum predicta domo, tenenda de Domino Rege pro .ij. *s.* per annum; unde habet cartam Regis, sicut aiunt juratores. Filius suus primogenitus est .xx. annorum, et habet filiam desponsatam .xviij. annorum et puellam .xvj. annorum et .ij. moniales et .ij. alias juniores.

45. Matillis, uxor Ingelram' de Dumard', est de donatione Domini Regis, et est plusquam .xl. annorum, et nullum habet heredem de Ingelram. Ipsa habet in dote tertiam partem de Faxton', que pars valet annuatim .vij. *l.* et .vj. *s.* et .viij. *.d.*

Hundredum de Wilebroc

46. Margareta Engaine fuit in donatione Domini Regis intra hos .viij. annos; et Galfridus Brito desponsavit eam, ut dicitur, sine licencia Regis; et hoc fuit prius ostensum justiciis. Galfridus Brito invenit plegios habendi warantum suum .iiij. septimanis post festum Sancti Michaelis, ad Scheccarium, de dicta Margareta quam duxit in uxorem, scilicet, Thomam de Hale et Alanum de Hale et Johannem de Sudwic.

Marginal note: Nota: placitum

and beyond the borough £7 2s 3d from fixed rents, which he holds from many years ago, not counting the land he holds in Upton of the Lord King.

44. Emma, widow of Hugh fitz Robert,[68] and before that widow of Robert of Saint Paul, and daughter of Henry Tiart, is in the Lord King's gift and is 40 years old. From Robert of Saint Paul she has dower in Oxfordshire worth 50s; and 63s from her marriage portion in Brington,[69] with stock of two plough-teams, 100 sheep, and 3 sows. Moreover, she also holds in dower one house in Northampton of the gift of Robert of Saint Paul, which is worth £8 per annum.[70] The Lord King gave the said woman in marriage to Hugh fitz Robert together with the said house to be held of the Lord King for 2s per annum, for which, according to the jurors, she has a royal charter. Her eldest son is 20 and she has a married daughter of 18, a daughter of 16, two daughters who are nuns, and two other younger daughters.

(Mawsley Hundred)

45. Matilda, widow of Ingelram de Dumard, is in the Lord King's gift and is more than 40 years of age and has no heir of Ingelram. She has one-third of Faxton in dower, which is worth £7 6s 8d.

Willybrook Hundred

46. Margaret Engaine has been in the Lord King's gift for the past eight years; and, according to the jurors, Geoffrey Brito married her without royal licence; and this was previously demonstrated to the justices. Geoffrey Brito has pledged sureties to produce his warrant three weeks after Michaelmas at the Exchequer, in the matter relating to the said Margaret whom he married, viz. Thomas of Hale, Alan of Hale, and John of Southwick.[71]

(*Marginal note*: note: a plea)

---

[68] The father of Robert fitz Hugh in the previous entry.

[69] Nobottle Hundred.

[70] This seems to be an extraordinarily high valuation for one house.

[71] This entry emphasises the importance of producing a warrant before the justices for marrying a widow in the Lord King's gift. Apparently Geoffrey Brito lost the case. The Pipe Roll of the following year records that he was fined 20 marks, of which he had paid 5, *pro uxore quam duxit sine licentia regis cum esset de donatione ejus*: *Pipe Roll 32 Henry II*, 9, and xxii. Round, *RD*, 24, n. 1, argued that the property involved was (Wood) Newton in Willybrook Hundred. See no. 56, which records her male heir.

47. Alicia, que fuit uxor Fulconis de Lisoriis et soror Willelmi de Aubervill', est in donatione Domini Regis, et est .l. annorum; et habet .ij. filios milites et .ij. alios et .vj. filias maritatas et .iiij. filias maritandas, que sunt in custodia matris. Terra sua in Glaptorn valet .c. *s.* cum hoc instauramento, scilicet, .ij. carrucis et .vj. vaccis et .j. tauro et .xxx. porcis et .xl. ovibus. Terra sua in Abiton', que est dos ejus et in Hundredo de Spelho, valet .xiiij. *l.* annuatim.

Hundredum de Stokes

48. Sibilla, que fuit uxor Galfridi Ridel et soror Willelmi Mauduit, est de donatione Domini Regis, et est .l. annorum. Terra sua in Weston' cum molendino valet .lxv. *s.*, .j. *d.* minus; et in Sutton' habet de suis liberis hominibus, .liiij: *s.* de redditu, et .j. quadradantem (*sic*). Ipsa habet .ij. filios et .j. filiam, sed non sunt heredes de dote ejus, sed Ricardus Basset qui fuit de prima uxore viri sui.

49. Alicia, que fuit uxor Thome de Bellofago et filia Waleranni de Oiri, est in donatione Domini Regis, et est .xx. annorum. Ipsa habet in Esselia feodum .j. militis et dimidium, quod Petrus de Esseleia et Robertus de Wateruill' tenent de ea; quorum servitium datum fuit in dote predicte domine. Ipsa habet .j. filium qui est .iiij. annorum, et est in custodia Nigelli filii Alexandri. Et preterea ipsa habet in Straton' .xx. libratas.[xi]

Hundredum de Hockeslawe

50. Ysowda, que fuit uxor Stephani de Bellocampo et filia comitis de Ferrariis, est in donatione Domini Regis, et est .xl. annorum. Ipsa habet in Bernewelle .x. libratas terre de feodo comitis in maritagio, et alias habet terras in comitatu de

---

[xi] This section has been underlined as if for deletion; it also appears to have been added later than the main entry.

47. Alice, widow of Fulk de Lisures and sister of William of Auberville, is in the Lord King's gift and is 50. She has two sons who are knights, and two others, six married daughters, and three daughters yet to be married, who are in their mother's wardship. Her land in Glapthorne is worth 100s with the following stock: viz. 2 plough-teams, 6 cows, one bull, 30 pigs, and 40 sheep. Her land in Abington, which is her dower in Spelho Hundred, is worth £14 per annum.[72]

Stoke Hundred

48. Sybil (Mauduit), widow of Geoffrey Ridel[73] and sister of William Mauduit, is in the Lord King's gift and is 50 years of age. Her land in Weston with the mill is worth 64s 11d; and in Sutton she has 54s in rent from her own freemen, and one farthing. She has two sons and one daughter, but they are not heirs to her dower, but Richard Basset (is) who was (the issue) of her husband's first wife.[74]

49. Alice, widow of Thomas de Belfou and daughter of Waleran d'Oiri, is in the Lord King's gift and is 20 years of age. She has one and a half knights' fees in Ashley,[75] which Peter of Ashley and Robert of Waterville hold of her, whose service was given to her in her dower. She has one son who is three years old and he is in the wardship of Nigel fitz Alexander.[76] Furthermore she has 20 librates in Stratton.[77]

Huxlow Hundred

50. Ysoude, widow of Stephen de Beauchamp and daughter of the earl of Ferrers, is in the Lord King's gift and is 40. She has 10 librates of land in Barnwell of the earl's fee as a marriage portion, and she has other estates in Worcestershire,

---

[72] With 13 children this is one of the two largest families in the *Rotuli*; the other is in entry no. 68.

[73] *Alias* Geoffey Basset, son of Richard Basset, the justiciar: Round, *RD*, xxxvi.

[74] The stepson from her husband's previous marriage takes priority. See no. 58.

[75] Round, *RD*, 25, n. 4, is wrong in placing Ashley (this entry) and Weston and Sutton (the preceding one) in Corby Hundred. They are, as the MS indicates, in Stoke Hundred. Likewise both Domesday Book and the Northamptonshire Survey of the Twelfth Century place these manors in Stoke Hundred: *Victoria County History* [hereafter *VCH*] *for Northamptonshire*, 2: 334–35, 386.

[76] Alice's uncle: Round, *RD*, 25, n. 4. See also nos. 105, 140, and 141.

[77] Sentence in MS has been underlined as if for deletion. See also no. 105, where the son is recorded as two years of age, and no. 140, where he is two and a half.

Wircestr', quas tenet de Domino Rege. Ipsa habet .j. filium, qui est .iiij. annorum, et .v. filias.

Marginal note: d.

51. In villa de Yslepe est filius cujusdam militis .xv. annorum, qui est in custodia Albrici de Witleberia, per Thomam filium Bernard'. Idem Albricus habuit custodiam ejusdem pueri septem annis, et de terra ejus cepit .xxxij. *d.* annuatim. Idem puer habet de terra Roberti filii Albrici redditum .xx. *s.*; et de terra Geruasii de Sudburc redditum .iij. *s.*; et terra illa est sochagium.

52. In villa de Stanford est quidam puer .xviij. annorum, qui fuit in custodia abbatis de Selebi quando obiit, et nunc est in custodia Willelmi de Stanford, qui dedit ei filiam suam pro .c. *s.*, quos dedit Domino Regi per dominum Rannulfum de Glanuill'. Terra sua valet per annum .xxiiij. *s.* sine dominio suo, scilicet, .j. carrucata terre; et ipse reddit de terra sua annuatim Domino Regi .j. *m.* argenti.

Marginal note: d.

Cleile Hundredum

53. Beatricia, que fuit uxor Roberti Mantel, servientis Domini Regis de honore de Notingham, est de donatione Domini Regis, et est .xxx. annorum. Terra sua in Roddes, quam habet in dote, valet .xxx. *s.* per annum cum instauramento .j. carruce, et sunt ibi .vj. virgate. Ipsa habet .iij. filios et .j. filiam; primogenitus est .x. annorum et in custodia Roberti de Saucei, ut dicunt, per Regem. Alii pueri sunt cum matre.

54. Terra Hamundi filii Hamundi filii Meinfelini in Wike valet per annum .iiij. *l.* et .x. *s.*, cum hoc instauramento; scilicet, .ij. carrucis et .l. ovibus et .iiij. vaccis et .iiij. suibus et .j. verre; et quia nullum est ibi instauramentum, non valet nisi .xxxvij. *s.*

which she holds of the Lord King. She has one son, who is four years of age, and five daughters.[78]

(*Marginal note*: d.)

51. In the vill of Islip the fifteen-year old son of a certain knight is in the wardship of Aubrey of Whittlebury through Thomas fitz Bernard:[79] Aubrey had wardship of the boy for seven years and took 32d per annum from his land. The same boy has 20s rent from the land of Robert fitz Aubrey and 3s rent from the land of Gervase of Sudborough, and that land is socage land.[80]

(Guilsborough Hundred)

52. In the vill of Stanford (on Avon) an 18-year old boy was in ward to the abbot of Selby when the latter died, and now he is in the wardship of William of Stanford, who gave his daughter in marriage to him for 100s, which he paid the Lord King through Rannulf Glanvill.[81] His land, not counting demesne, is worth 24s per annum, viz. one carrucate of land. And he himself renders one mark of silver per annum from his land to the Lord King.

(*Marginal note*: d.)

Cleyley Hundred

53. Beatrice, widow of Robert Mantel, a royal serjeant of the honour of Nottingham, is in the Lord King's gift and is 30 years old. Her land in Roade, which she has in dower, is worth 30s per annum with stock of one plough-team, and there are six virgates there. She has three sons and one daughter. The eldest son is 10 years of age and is in the wardship of Robert de Saucei, so they say, by order of the King. The other children are with the mother.[82]

54. The land of Hamo, son of Hamo fitz Meinfelin, in Wicken is worth £4 10s per annum with the following stock, viz. 2 plough-teams, 50 sheep, 4 cows, 4 sows, and one boar; and because there is no stock there it is worth only 37s.[83]

---

[78] For further entries relating to Stephen de Beauchamp see nos. 147, 153, 173 (which records three daughters), and 200.

[79] Sheriff of Northamptonshire.

[80] Sudborough, Huxlow Hundred, Northants. Socage stressed the fiscal aspect of the soke and implied a money rent: Douglas, *The Social Structure of Medieval East Anglia*, 184.

[81] Selby Abbey was vacant on the death of Abbot Gilbert de Vere in 1184; therefore its temporalities were in the king's hand.

[82] See also no. 82.

[83] The sheriff accounted for 40s at the Exchequer: *Pipe Roll 31 Henry II*, 53. See also nos. 62 and 84. The caput of the barony was Wolverton in Buckinghamshire (no. 84).

55. Haddun', que est de honore comitis Leicestr', fuit in manu Domini Regis; et Radulfus Morinus cepit inde de lana et caseis .xx. *s.*, et .cc. oves et .xxx. et .j. ovem et .xxj. bovem et .v. averos. Radulfus de Wirecestre recepit .xv. *m.* de blado et feno, et de firma .xj. *m.* et .v. *s.* et .vj. *d.*, et de pomario .v. *s.* Dictam villam tradidit Dominus Rex Willelmo de Diua, et heredem, qui est .xij. annorum, et habet fratrem .v. annorum et .j. sororem .ix. annorum et aliam .vij.

Marginal note: d.

56. Margareta Engaine, quam desponsavit Gaufridus Brito, ut supradictum est, habet in Pictesleia .vj. libratas terre; et ipsa est .l. annorum et heres ejus est Ricardus Engaine. Et fuit filia Ricardi filii Ursi.

[Rot. 3. d.]

57. Albreia de Harwecurt est in donatione Domini Regis, et est .l. annorum, et habet .iiij. filios. Terra sua in Brantest', que est maritagium suum, valet per annum xiiij. *l.* cum instauramento .iiij. carrucarum et .iij.c. ovium. In eadem villa sunt .iiij. virgate terre cum pertinentiis que pertinent ad manerium Domini Regis de Faleweslea, et reddunt annuatim. xij. *s.* et .iiij. *d.*; et dicta Albreia tenet illas per voluntatem Domini Regis et cepit de terra .iiij. *l.* et .x. *s.*, preter firmam: et qui terram tenent, tenent eam[xii] libere et hereditarie.

[xii] There is a character between "eam" and "libere," which Sir Simonds D'Ewes interpreted as "s(cilicet)": Harl. MS 624, fol. 152v. It has been omitted altogether from the editions of Grimaldi (*Rotuli de Dominabus*, 14) and Round (*RD*, 28), possibly because the passage makes better sense that way or because it was seen as a clumsy attempt to erase a punctus elevatus.

(Nobottle Hundred)

55. (East) Haddon, which belongs to the honour of the earl of Leicester, was in the Lord King's hand, and Ralph Morin[84] took from there 20s from wool and cheese, 231 sheep, 21 oxen, and 5 farm-horses. Ralph of Worcester received 15 marks from grain and hay, 11 marks, 5s 6d from the farm of the manor, and 5s from the orchard. The Lord King handed over the said vill to William de Dives together with the heir, who is 12 years of age. He has a brother aged 5, one sister aged 9 and another aged 7.[85]

(*Marginal note*: d.)

(Orlingbury Hundred)

56. Margaret Engaine, whom Geoffrey Brito married, as has been said above, has 6 librates of land in Pytchley, and she is 50, and her heir is Richard Engaine. She was the daughter of Richard fitz Urse.[86]

[Roll 3. dorse.]

(Gravesend Hundred)

57. Aubrey de Harcourt is in the Lord King's gift, is 50 years old, and has four sons. Her land in Braunston, which is her marriage portion, is worth £14 per annum with stock of 4 plough-teams and 300 sheep. In the same vill there are 4 virgates of land with appurtenances, which belong to the Lord King's manor of Fawsley and they render 12s 4d per annum. The said Aubrey holds them at the King's will and took from the land £4 10s besides the farm: and those who hold land (there) hold it freely and hereditarily.[87]

---

[84] Ralph Morin had recently replaced Thomas fitz Bernard as sheriff of Northamptonshire.

[85] The earl of Leicester's lands had been seized by the Crown as a result of the 1183 rebellion. They were restored to the earl in the following year. The ages of all the children are given in this entry.

[86] See no. 46. The Engaine family held land at Pytchley for the service of clearing the forest of wolves: Poole, *Domesday Book to Magna Carta*, 31.

[87] Aubrey de Harcourt was the wife of William Trussebut (d. 1175–76) and mother of Rose, the subject of entry no. 1. Only the four sons are mentioned in this entry. According to the *Liber Memorandorum Ecclesie de Bernewelle*, 48, Aubrey had five sons and three daughters. However, see Clay, *Early Yorkshire Charters*, 10: 11, n. 1, where doubt is cast on the trustworthiness of the *Liber Memorandorum*.

58. Sibilla, que fuit uxor Gaufridi Ridel et soror Willelmi Mauduit, habet in Frixton' .xx. libratas terre, quas Gaufridus Basset ei dedit in dotem, de quibus Ricardus Basset est heres.

59. Matillis Gulaffre, que fuit filia Rogeri Gulaffre et soror Hereberti Gulaffre, est de donatione Domini Regis, et est .lx. annorum. Ipsa habet de Willelmo de Curci .xl. solidatas terre in hundredo de Norton', et .iiij. libratas habuit in dote in Parva Blakewell', de honore de Notingham, quam ipsa reddidit Ricardo filio suo elapsis .iij. annis. Ipsa habet .iij. filios et .ij. filias, et heres ejus est miles; et per dictam terram est de donatione Domini Regis.

Duo Hundreda de Sutton'

60. Heres Gileberti de Monte et filius fuit in custodia Thome filii Bernardi, cum .iiij. sororibus suis et terra sua, elapsis .viij. annis, scilicet, postquam reddidit se in monasterio de Einesham. Nunc autem heres est in custodia Galfridi filii Petri cum terra sua, et .iii. sorores ejus et mater. Quarta maritata est cuidam libero homini de feodo illo, per donationem Thome filii Bernardi. Heres est .xv. annorum, et fuit nepos Thome de Sancto Johanne et Johannis de Sancto Johanne et Hugonis de Plugenet et Willelmi Fossard'. Terra ejus valet annuatim de asiso redditu .iiij. *l.* et dim. et .vj. *s.* et .v. *d.*; et hunc redditum recepit Thomas filius Bernardi dum habuit custodiam. Et cum rationabili instauramento, scilicet, .ij. carrucarum et .c. ovium et .iiij. vaccarum et .j. tauri et .iiij. suum et .j. verris, terra sua in Hwitefeld' valeret .viij. *l.* et dim. et .v. *d.*; et non sunt ibi modo nisi due carruce de dicto instauramento. Johannes clericus qui tunc fuit senescallus Thome filii Bernardi, tradidit villate de Hwitefeld' .xl. hogastros ad festum Sancti Martini, et cepit[xiii] totidem[xiv] bonas matrices oves ad Pascha pro eis, injuste, cum agnis; et preterea cepit .xvj. tinatas cervisie, quarum quelibet valebat .ij. *d.*, pro quibus

---

[xiii] Not "recepit" as in Round, *RD*, 29, and in Harl. MS 624.
[xiv] Corrected from "toditem" in MS.

58. Sybil, widow of Geoffrey Ridel and sister of William Mauduit, holds 20 librates in *Frixton*,[88] which Geoffrey Basset gave her as dower, and to which Richard Basset is the heir.[89]

(Norton Hundred)[90]

59. Matilda Gulafre, daughter of Roger Gulafre and sister of Herbert Gulafre, is in the Lord King's gift and is 60 years of age. She holds 40 solidates of land of William de Courcy in the hundred of Norton, and she held 4 librates of land in dower at Little Blakesley of the honour of Nottingham, which she returned to her son Richard three years ago. She has three sons and two daughters, and her heir is a knight; and by virtue of the said land she is in the Lord King's gift.

The Double Hundred of Sutton[91]

60. The son and heir of Gilbert de Mont was in ward to Thomas fitz Bernard, together with his four sisters and his land, for eight years, that is after he (Gilbert) retired to the monastery of Eynsham. But now the heir is in the wardship of Geoffrey fitz Peter, together with his land, and three of his sisters and his mother. The fourth sister married a certain freeman of that fee by the gift of Thomas fitz Bernard. The heir is 15 years of age and was a nephew of Thomas and John of Saint John, Hugh de Plugenoi, and William Fossard. His land is worth £4 16s 5d per annum in fixed rents; and Thomas fitz Bernard received this rent whilst he had wardship. With reasonable stock, viz. 2 plough-teams, 100 sheep, 4 cows, one bull, 4 sows, and one boar, his land at Whitfield would be worth £8 10s 5d. And there is none of the above stock there now except for the 2 plough-teams. John, the clerk, who was at that time Thomas fitz Bernard's steward, transferred 40 hoggets[92] to the vill of Whitfield at the feast of Saint Martin (11 November) and unjustly took as many good ewes for them at Easter together with their lambs. Furthermore, he took 16 casks of beer, each of which was worth 2d, for

---

[88] According to Round, *RD*, 28, n. 2, this was either Strixton in Higham Ferrers Hundred or Faxton in Orlingbury Hundred.

[89] See no. 48. Geoffrey Ridel and Geoffrey Basset are one and the same: Round, *RD*, xxxvi. He died in 1180: Sanders, *English Baronies*, 49.

[90] This was Foxley Hundred at the time of Domesday Book. The Gulafres held land in Adston and Green's Norton in this hundred.

[91] The double hundred of Sutton was the result of the almagamation of the hundreds of Sutton and Alboldstow.

[92] Two-year-old male sheep.

nichil reddidit; et preter firmam cepit .j. bovem, et Radulfus Morinus dimidiam marcam de quodam homine de villa. Custodes Thome filii Bernardi ceperunt intra hos .viij. annos, .v. *l.* et dimidiam de villa preter firmam, et .viij. *s.* injuste.

Marginal note: d.[xv]

61. Alicia de Essex est de donatione Domini Regis, et est .lx. annorum, et est amita Comitis Willelmi, et soror Comitis Albrici, et habet .ij. filios milites, et .j. filiam maritatam Johanni constabulario Cestrie. Arenho quod est manerium ejus, quod etiam tenet de Comite Willelmo, valet annuatim .xxx. *l.*, cum hoc instauramento, scilicet, .iiij. carrucis et .cccc. ovibus et cum .vj. suibus et .vij. hogastris; sed quia .ccc. oves deficiunt, terra non valet nisi .xxvij. *l.*

62. Terra que fuit Hamonis Meinfelin' in Tanford' est seisita in manum Domini Regis; sed nichil inde captum fuit postquam fuit in manum Domini Regis, et valet annuatim .viij. *l.* cum rationabili instauramento.

Marginal note: d.[xvi]

At the foot of the roll: Norhant'sir' p

[Rot. 4.]

Hic est rotulus de dominabus et puellis que sunt de donatione Domini Regis in Bedefordsire et de pueris; et de Bukinghamsire

Primo de Bedef' et postea de Bukingh', demum de Huntedun'sire

Hundredum De Bereford

63. Alda, que est filia Hugonis de Bellocampo et fuit uxor Willelmi Maubanc, est de donatione Domini Regis, et est .xxx. annorum; et habet .iiij. filias, quarum primogenita est .xvj. annorum, et in custodia Hugonis de Bellocampo. Cokesdune,

---

[xv] Omitted from Round, *RD*, 29.
[xvi] Omitted from Round, *RD*, 30.

which he paid nothing. And beside the farm he took one ox, and Ralph Morin (took) half a mark from a certain man of the vill. In these eight years the custodians of Thomas fitz Bernard unjustly took £5 18s in addition to the farm.[93]

(*Marginal note*: d.)

61. Alice of Essex is in the Lord King's gift, is 60 years old, and is an aunt of Earl William (de Mandeville, earl of Essex), and a sister of Earl Aubrey (de Vere, earl of Oxford).[94] She has two sons who are knights, and one daughter, who is married to John (fitz Eustace), constable of Chester. Her manor of Aynho, which she also holds of Earl William, is worth £30 per annum with the following stock: viz. 4 plough-teams, 400 sheep, 6 sows, and 7 hoggets, but because there is a shortfall of 300 sheep the estate is worth only £27.[95]

62. Hamo Meinfelin's land in Thenford was seized into the Lord King's hand; but nothing was taken from it after it was in the King's possession. It is worth £8 per annum with reasonable stock.[96]

(*Marginal note*: d.)

At the foot of the roll: Northamptonshire p'.

[Roll 4.]

This is the roll concerning ladies and girls who are in the Lord King's gift in Bedfordshire and concerning boys; and of Buckinghamshire.

First concerning Bedfordshire, then Buckinghamshire, finally Huntingdonshire

Barford Hundred

63. Alda, daughter of Hugh de Beauchamp and widow of William Maubanc, is in the Lord King's gift. She is 30 and has four daughters, of whom the eldest is 16 and in the wardship of Hugh de Beauchamp. Roxton, which is her marriage

---

[93] This entry is discussed in Lally, "Secular Patronage," 163–64.

[94] For the links between the Mandevilles and the de Veres see J. H. Round, *Geoffrey de Mandeville* (London, 1892), 388–96. The manor of Aynho was granted by William de Mandeville to Alice of Essex over and above her husband's dower.

[95] This is the first of many examples of the equation that 100 sheep were worth £1 to the annual value of the estate. See also nos. 69, 70, 90, 99, 109, 111, and 144. For more on Alice of Essex, see no. 191, where she is recorded as 80 years old.

[96] See nos. 54 and 84.

quod est maritagium ejus, valet annuatim .ix. *l.* Et cum .iij. carrucis et .c. ovibus et .v. vaccis et .j. tauro, .v. suibus et .j. verre, valeret .xij. *l.*

Hundredum de Wigstanetre

64. Maria de Traili, que fuit uxor Gaufridi de Traili, est de donatione Domini Regis, et est .xl. annorum, et fuit cognata Comitis Simonis. Walterus de Traili est filius ejus et heres, et preter eum habet alium filium monachum, et .j. filiam maritatam, et aliam monialem. Terra sua, scilicet, Northgile, valet annuatim .xiiij. *l.*

Hundredum de Clifton'

65. Matillis de Kaineto est in donatione Domini Regis, et habet .ij. filios. Primogenitus est .xviij. annorum, alter .xij. Terra sua in Kamelton' valet .vij. *l.* annuatim.

66. Petrus filius Roberti de Suriue est in custodia Willelmi Comitis per Dominum Regem, et est .xv. annorum, et habet ij. hidas terre in Wimedune, quas Wischardus Leddet tenet per Willelmum Comitem. Et dicta terra valet annuatim .xl. *s.* Et cum instauramento .j. carruce et .xl. ovium et .iiij. vaccarum et .ij. suum valeret terra .iiij. *m.* per annum.

Hundredum de Bekeleswad'

67. Gaufridus, filius Roberti, camerarii, fuit et est in custodia Gaufridi filii Azonis cum tribus sororibus et fratre suo. Predictus Gaufridus habet . . . . . .annos etatis. Duniton', villa predicti Gaufridi, valet annuatim .xv. *l.* cum hoc instauramento, scilicet, .xij. bobus et .iiij. averis et .j. vitulo, .iiij. suibus et .j. verre, .iiij.[xx] ovibus duabus minus. Hoc instauramentum receperunt homines de predicta villa quando

portion, is worth £9 per annum, but with 3 plough-teams, 100 sheep, 5 cows, one bull, 5 sows, and one boar could be worth £12. [97]

Wixamtree Hundred

64. Mary de Trailly, widow of Geoffrey de Trailly, is in the Lord King's gift. She is 40 and was a cousin of Earl Simon (of Northamptonshire). Walter de Trailly is her son and heir, and apart from him she has another son, who is a monk, a married daughter, and another daughter, who is a nun. Her land, viz. Northill, is worth £14 per annum.

Clifton Hundred

65. Matilda de Chesney is in the Lord King's gift and she has two sons. The elder is 18, the other 12. Her land in Campton is worth £7 per annum.[98]

(Willey Hundred)

66. Peter fitz Robert de Surive is in the wardship of Earl William (of Essex) through the Lord King and is 15 years of age. He has 2 hides of land in Wymington, which Wischard Leddet holds through Earl William. The said land is worth 40s per annum. With stock of one plough-team, 40 sheep, 4 cows, and 2 sows the land would be worth 4 marks per annum.

Biggleswade Hundred

67. Geoffrey fitz Robert, the chamberlain, was and is in the wardship of Geoffrey fitz Azo, together with his three sisters and his brother. The former Geoffrey is . . .[99] years of age. His vill of Dunton is worth £15 per annum with the following stock: viz. 12 oxen, 4 farm-horses, one calf, 4 sows, one bull, and 78 sheep. The men of the vill received this stock when they received the vill at farm from

---

[97] The Beauchamps possessed the barony of Bedford and the Maubancs were the palatinate barons of Chester. Round, *RD*, 31, n. 1, argues that "Cokesdune" in Barford Hundred is the "Rochesdune" of Domesday Book. As Herlihy has pointed out, Alda must have been younger than 14 when she married: Herlihy, *Medieval Households*, 105.

[98] *Pipe Roll 30 Henry II*, 72, records Matilda paying a total of 300 marks for possession of her land and wardship of her son's land.

[99] The number has simply been omitted. There is no blank or damage to the MS.

receperunt villam ad firmam a Gaufrido filio Azonis. Predictus Gaufridus filius Azonis cepit preter firmam, postquam habuit custodiam, de releviis et aliis exitibus, .xiij. *l.* et .x. *s.*

Hundredum De Flete

68. Beatricia, que fuit uxor Ricardi Gubiun, est de donatione Domini Regis, sicut creditur, quia habet dotem suam in Norhamt', et ipsa est .xl. annorum et eo amplius, et habet .vij. filios et .vj. filias. Ipsa habet in hundredo de Flete de feodo Simonis de Bellocampo .xviij. libratas terre.

Hundredum de Manesheue

69. Matillis Malaherba est in donatione Domini Regis, et est .xl. annorum; et filium heredem militem habet, et preter eum filios et filias, et nescitur a juratoribus quot. Medietas ville de Hoccliue, que est maritagium suum, quam tenet de Roberto Malherbe, fratre suo, valet annuatim .iiij. *l.* et .xv. *s.* et .iiij. *d.*, cum .j. carruca que est ibi; et si apponerenter .c. oves, valeret .c. et .xv. *s.* et .iiij. *d.*

Chalgraue[xvii]

70. Chalgraue, que fuit hereditas Rogeri le Lohereng', post mortem ejus, fuit in manu Philippi de Windesor' .v. annis et dimidio pro .c. et .iij. *m.*, quas dictus Philippus dedit Simoni de Bellocampo, scilicet, domino feodi, ut haberet custodiam dicte terre cum heredibus Rogeri .xviij. annis.[xviii] Post mortem Philippi Amaurius suscepit eandem custodiam per Dominum Regem ad eundem terminum, et jam tenuit per .ij. annos et dimidium. Petrus, heres predicti Rogeri, erit .xij. annorum ad proximum Pascha. Villa predicta cum pertinenciis valet .xxij. *l.* et .v. *s.*, cum instauramento quod ibi est. Domina Akina habet inter .x. libratas. Preterea Willelmus Lohareng' reddit manerio .j. sprevarium sorum. Et Willelmus filius Hugonis, .j. libram piperis. Et si .iij..c. oves apponerentur, redditus manerii posset crescere in .lx. *s.*

[xvii] Entered as if a hundred, but Chalgrave was in Manshead Hundred.

[xviii] Round, *RD*, 34, n. 1, quite rightly argued for a sentence break here. There is in fact a hint of a period after "annis."

Geoffrey fitz Azo.[100] Besides the farm Geoffrey fitz Azo took £13 10s from reliefs and other issues after he had wardship.

Flitt Hundred

68. Beatrice, widow of Richard Gubiun, is in the Lord King's gift, so it is believed, because she has her dower in Northampton. She is more than 40 years old, and has seven sons and six daughters. In Flitt Hundred she has 18 librates of land[101] of the fee of Simon de Beauchamp.

Manshead Hundred

69. Matilda Malherbe is in the Lord King's gift and is 40. She has a son who is a knight and her heir, and besides him she has (other) sons and daughters, but the jurors do not know how many. Half the vill of Hockcliffe, which is her marriage portion, and which she holds of her brother, Robert Malherbe, is worth £4 15s 4d per annum with one plough-team, which is there; and if 100 sheep were added it would be worth £5 15s 4d.

Chalgrave[102]

70. Chalgrave, which was the inheritance of Roger de Lohereng, was in Philip of Windsor's hand for five and a half years after his (Roger's) death for 103 marks, which the said Philip gave to Simon de Beauchamp, the lord of the fee, so that he might have wardship of the said land, together with Roger's heirs for 18 years. After Philip's death Amaurius took over the same wardship through the Lord King for the same term, and he has held it now for two and a half years. Peter, the above Roger's heir, will be 12 years of age next Easter. The said vill with its appurtenances is worth £22 5s with the existing stock. Lady Akina has approximately ten librates.[103] Furthermore, William Lohereng renders one unmewed sparrowhawk for the manor, and William fitz Hugh, one pound of pepper. And if 300 sheep were placed there the return of the manor could be increased by 60s.

---

[100] A good example of collective farming by the men of the vill. See also no. 105. Geoffrey fitz Azo was sheriff of Hampshire, 1179–1189.

[101] Possibly at Higham Gobion.

[102] Erroneously prefixed as if it were an hundredal heading. Chalgrave was in Manshead Hundred.

[103] Lady Akina was probably the widow. Ten librates represents almost two-fifths of the potential value of the estate.

Bukinghamsire. Rotulus de dominabus et puellis que sunt de donatione Domini Regis, et de pueris qui sunt in ejus custodia in Bukinghamsire

Hundredum de Coteslawe

71. Filia Walteri de Bolebec, que fuit .ix. annorum a festo Sancti Michaelis, et[xix] fuit in custodia Comitis Albrici post inicium Quadragesime. Terra sua de Hwitchirche, que est de feodo Walteri de Bolebec, fuit in custodia Reginaldi de Curtenei .ix. annis elapsis a festo Sancti Johannis; et valet annuatim .xx. *l.*, sine auxiliis et dominio et gardina cum hoc instauramento, scilicet, .iij. carrucis et .j. verre et .v. suibus et .xxj. purcello (*sic*).

Hundredum de Stokes

72. Willelmus de Windesor', filius Willelmi de Windesor' senioris, est in custodia Domini Regis. Et per eum est et fuit in custodia Hawis de Windesor', matris sue, per .ix.[xx] annos, cum terra sua, scilicet, Horton' et Eton'. Predictus Willelmus est .xviij. annorum. Horton' valet annuatim, .xiiij. *l.*, cum hoc instauramento, scilicet, .ij. carrucis de .xvij. bobus, et .iiij. averis, .v. suibus, .j. verre, .v. vaccis et .j. tauro. Eton' valet anuatim (*sic*) .x. *l.*, cum hoc instauramento, scilicet, .j. carruca de .viij. bobus et .j. avero et .ij. vaccis proinde.[xxi]

73. Hawis de Windesor' est de donatione Domini Regis, et preter heredem suum prenominatum, habet .vij. filias, quarum .ij. sunt in transmarinis partibus, .ij. sunt moniales, .iij. sunt in donatione Domini Regis. Etas dicte domine ignoratur a juratoribus, quia nata fuit in transmarinis partibus.

74. Tres filie Stephani forestarii sunt in donatione Domini Regis in villa de Heure. Galfridus de Bosco habet matrem illarum et illas sorores in custodia cum dimidia virgata terre que est hereditas illarum in villa de Heuere, per Thomam Basset: et defendit illam dimidiam virgatam terre per servicium militis quantum pertinet ad dimidiam virgatam terre; et valet dicta terra dimidiam marcam.

[xix] Omitted from Round, *RD*, 34.

[xx] This may well be "x." There is a heavy smudge mark before "x." The probability that it was meant to be ".ix." is confirmed by entry no. 87.

[xxi] The final word is omitted from the editions of Grimaldi (*Rotuli de Dominabus*, 18), and Round (*RD*, 35), but not from Harl. MS 624, fol. 153v, where it appears as "p'dc.". It is probably meant to be "p(roin)de."

Buckinghamshire. Roll concerning ladies and girls who are in the Lord King's gift, and concerning boys who are in his wardship in Buckinghamshire

Cottesloe Hundred

71. The daughter of Walter of Bolbec, who was nine years of age at Michaelmas, was in the wardship of Earl Aubrey from the beginning of Lent. Her land of Whitchurch, which belongs to the fee of Walter of Bolbec, has been in the wardship of Reginald de Courtenay since the feast of St. John (24 June) nine years ago; and it is worth £20 per annum, not counting aids, demesne, and the garden, with the following stock: viz. 3 plough-teams, one boar, 5 sows, and 21 piglets.[104]

Stoke Hundred

72. William of Windsor, son of William of Windsor senior, is in ward to the Lord King, and through him he is and has been in the wardship of his mother, Hawise of Windsor, for 9 years, together with his land, viz. Horton and Eton. The said William is 18 years old. Horton is worth £14 per annum with the following stock: viz. 2 plough-teams with 17 oxen, 4 farm-horses, 5 sows, one boar, 5 cows, and one bull. Eton is worth £10 per annum with the following stock: viz. one plough-team of 8 oxen, one farm-horse, and 2 cows.[105]

73. Hawise of Windsor is in the Lord King's gift and besides the aforenamed heir has seven daughters, of whom two are overseas, two are nuns, and three are in the Lord King's gift. The widow's age is not known by the jurors because she was born overseas.[106]

74. The three daughters of Stephen, the forester, are in the Lord King's gift in the vill of Iver. Geoffrey de Bosco has their mother and the sisters in wardship with half a virgate of land, which is their inheritance in the vill of Iver, through Thomas Basset, and he (Geoffrey) answers for that half-virgate of land with the knight-service due from a half-virgate. The said land is worth half a mark.

---

[104] See also nos. 89 and 223, where she appears as a ten-year-old. The wardship of the heiress (Isabel) and the wardship of the land appear to be in separate hands, as seems to be the case in no. 111. She later married her custodian, Earl Aubrey II: Round, *RD*, xli, and Sanders, *English Baronies*, 98.

[105] For the Windsor family see nos. 73, 87, and 228.

[106] According to no. 228 she had six daughters.

[Rot. 4. d.]

Hundredum De Ruelaue

75. Filia Walteri de Burton' est de donatione Domini Regis et tenet dimidiam hidam terre in Burton', quam pater suus tenuit per serianteriam dispensarie, et ipsa est .x. annorum.

Marginal note: d.[xxii]

Hundredum de Dusteberge

76. In Wicumba terra que fuit Ginant fuit in manu Domini Regis cum Elia filio et herede ipsius, et .ij. filiabus ejusdem hiis .viij. annis; et heres ipsius est .xvij. annorum, et .j. filia .xviij. annorum, et altera .xiiij. Dicta terra cum herede fuit in custodia Alexandri medarii .viij. annis per Dominum Regem; et terra sine instauramento valet .iij. *m.*, quas dictus Alexander annuatim recepit. Et cum hoc instauramento, scilicet, .viij. bobus, .ij. averis, .ij. vaccis et .lx. ovibus et .vj. porcis, valeret annuatim .v. *m.*; et terra non potest plus instauramenti pati, et defendit se pro quinta parte militis. Et preterea tenet heres .j. virgatam terre de feodo Wicumbie pro .vij. *s.*, et .j. acram pro .ij. *s.* et .iij. *d.*, que valet amplius .xiij. *d.* annuatim. Hiis .viij. annis cepit dictus Alexander de dicta terra .iiij. *m.* de proficuo.

Marginal note: d.

77. Filius Angoti filii Anketilli de Wicumbe, qui est .xiij. annorum, est in custodia Domini Regis, et per eum in custodia Matildis matris sue per finem quam fecit cum Domino Rege pro .xl. *m.* Et habet dictus heres, scilicet, Robertus, .iij. fratres et .iiij. sorores, quarum primogenita est .xvj. annorum. Terra sua in Wicumb', que se defendit pro feodo dimidii militis, valet annuatim .c. *s.*, cum hoc instauramento, scilicet, .ij. carrucis de .xij. bobus, et .iiij. averis et .ij. juvenculis et .iiij.[xx] ovibus et .ij. equis; nec potest plus instauramenti pati nec plus terra valere. Preterea filius filius (*sic*) Angoti habet molendinum quod pertinet ad feodum de Wicumba, de quo solvit .xxx. *s.*, et .iiij. acras et dimidiam de burgagio, unde solvit .vj. *s.* et dimidium. Et superplussagium valet ei .ij. *s.* et .vj. *d.*

78. Matildis, uxor dicti Angoti, est .xxx. annorum et fuit filia Roberti de Hauechford'; et tenet quandam terram de Roberto de Rotomago, de qua reddit .xxviij. *d.*, et valet preterea annuatim .xv. *s.*

Marginal note: d.[xxiii]

[xxii] Omitted from Round, *RD*, 36.
[xxiii] Omitted from Round, *RD*, 37.

[Roll 4. dorse.]

Rowley Hundred

75. The daughter of Walter of Bourton is in the Lord King's gift and holds half a hide of land in Bourton, which her father held by serjeanty as a steward; and she is 10 years of age.[107]

(*Marginal note*: d.)

Desborough Hundred

76. Ginant's land in Wycombe has been in the Lord King's hand, together with Elias, his son and heir, and his two daughters, for these (past) eight years. His heir is 17 years old; one daughter is 18, and the other 14. The said land with the heir was in the wardship of Alexander, the mead steward, for eight years through the Lord King, and without stock it is worth 3 marks, which Alexander received annually. With the following stock of 8 oxen, 2 farm-horses, 2 cows, 60 sheep, and 6 pigs it would be worth 5 marks per annum. The land is unable to sustain more stock and is answerable for one-fifth of a knight's fee. In addition, the heir has one virgate of land of the fee of Wycombe for 7s (per annum) and one acre for 2s 3d, which is worth 13d more per annum. In these (last) eight years Alexander took 4 marks from the proceeds of the land.

(*Marginal note*: d.)

77. The son of Angot fitz Anketill of Wycombe, who is 13, is in ward to the Lord King, and through him is in the wardship of Matilda, his mother, for a fine of 40 marks, which she has paid to the Lord King.[108] The said heir, namely Robert, has three brothers and four sisters, and the eldest sister is 16. His land in Wycombe, which is answerable for half a knight's fee, is worth 100s per annum with the following stock: viz. 2 plough-teams with 12 oxen, 4 farm-horses, 2 heifers, 80 sheep, and 2 horses. Nor is it possible to sustain more stock or for the land to be worth more. Furthermore, Angot's son has a mill which belongs to the fee of Wycombe, for which he pays 30s, and 3½ burgage acres, for which he pays 6s 6d. And the surplus is worth 2s 6d. to him.

78. Matilda, widow of the above Angot, is 30 and was the daughter of Robert de *Hauechford* and she holds some land of Robert of Rouen from which she renders 28d and it is worth 15s per annum more than this.

(*Marginal note*: d.)

---

[107] See no. 95.
[108] The payment is recorded in *Pipe Roll 31 Henry II*, 140, and *Pipe Roll 32 Henry II*, 27.

79. In Wicumba uxor Rogeri Pinel, que est .xxv. annorum, et fuit filia Jordani de Ratdene, est in donatione Domini Regis; nec habet aliquam prolem, et habet terciam partem dimidie hide terre in dote.

80. Basilia, que fuit uxor David Pinel fratris dicti Rogeri, et est .xviij. annorum, et fuit filia Roberti Tailard' de Merlawe, est in donatione Domini Regis; et habet .ij. partes dicte dimidie hide terre, cum pueris suis, scilicet, .j. filio et .j. filia, qui sunt in custodia matris . . . . . .per Gilebertum Basset; et est filius .iiij. annorum, filia .ij. annorum. Dicta dimidia hida duarum viduarum valet annuatim .xxx. *s.*, cum hoc instauramento, scilicet, .viij. bobus et .ij. averis et .l. ovibus et .vj. porcis. Preterea dicte vidue tenent .j. virgatam terre de Gileberto Pipart pro .j. hospitio per annum. Preterea, heres David tenet .j. acram terre de Thoma de Sancto Johanne, de qua solvit .ij. *s.* per annum, et valet sibi preterea .xxxij. *d.* per annum; et dimidiam acram tenet de burgo pro .xij. *d.*, de qua recipit preterea .ij. *s.* Rogerus Pinel obiit elapsis .v. annis a Pascha, et David elapso .j. anno, et postea vixerunt vidue vix de exitibus predicte terre.

81. Willelmus, qui fuit filius Willelmi de Noers filii Hugonis, est .xviij. annorum, et in custodia Henrici de Pinkeni, cujus filiam desponsavit per Dominum Regem elapsis jam .iiij. annis. Terra sua in Messedena valet annuatim .xv. *l.* cum hoc instauramento, scilicet, .ij. carrucis, .c. ovibus, .v vaccis, .j. tauro, .xx. porcis. Henricus cepit de villa postquam habuit eam .xxxviii. *l.* et .xiiij. *s.* de redditibus, de dono hominum .xij. *m.*, de placitis .iiij. *m.*, de nemore .iij. *m.*

82. Filius Roberti Mantelli, qui est .x. annorum, est in custodia Domini Regis et habet dimidiam hidam terre in Messeden', que est in custodia Roberti de Sawcia, et valet annuatim .xx. *s.* Filius Roberti Mantell' habet .ij. fratres et .j. sororem.

Hundredum de Stanes

83. Agnes de Muntchenesy est de donatione Domini Regis, et villa sua de Dunton' valet annuatim .xxij. *l.* cum hoc instauramento, scilicet, .iij. carrucis, .cc. ovibus, .iiij. vaccis, .j. tauro, .iiij. suibus et .j. verre.

79. In Wycombe the widow of Roger Pinel, who is 25 years of age and was the daughter of Jordan de *Ratdene*, is in the Lord King's gift. She does not have any heir, and she has one-third of half a hide in dower.

80. Basilia, widow of David Pinel, brother of the above Roger, is 18 years of age and was the daughter of Robert Tailard of Marlowe, and is in the Lord King's gift. She has two-thirds of the above half hide of land, with her children, one boy and one girl, who are in the wardship of (their) mother through Gilbert Basset. The son is 3 years of age, the daughter two. The half hide of the two widows is worth 30s per annum with the following stock: viz. 8 oxen, 2 farm-horses, 50 sheep, and 6 pigs. Furthermore, the two widows hold one virgate of land from Gilbert Pipart for one lodging[109] per annum. Moreover, the heir, David, holds one acre of land of Thomas of Saint John, for which he pays 2s per annum, and over and above this it is worth 32d per annum to him; and half an acre of borough (land) for 12d, from which, however, he receives a further 2s. Roger Pinel died 5 years ago at Easter and David one year ago. Thereafter the widows scarcely survived on the proceeds of the aforesaid land.

(Stone Hundred)

81. William, son of William de Noers son of Hugh, is 18 and in the wardship of Henry de Pinkney, whose daughter he married four years ago under royal licence. His land in Missenden is worth £15 per annum with the following stock: viz. 2 plough-teams, 100 sheep, 5 cows, one bull, and 20 pigs. After he received the vill Henry took £38 14s in rents from it, 12 marks from the men's gift,[110] 4 marks from pleas, and 3 marks from the wood.

82. The son of Robert Mantel, who is 10 years old, is in ward to the Lord King and he holds half a hide of land in Missenden, which is in the wardship of Robert de Saucei, and it is worth 20s per annum. The son of Robert Mantel has two brothers and one sister.[111]

Stone Hundred

83. Agnes de Mountchesney is in the Lord King's gift and her vill of Dinton is worth £22 with the following stock: viz. 3 plough-teams, 200 sheep, 4 cows, one bull, 4 sows, and one boar.[112]

---

[109] Probably one night's lodging.

[110] I.e. feudal aid.

[111] This was a serjeanty tenure, held by napery service: J. H. Round, *The King's Serjeants and Officers of State* (London, 1911), 225. See no. 53.

[112] See nos. 116, 126, 127, and 143.

Hundredum de Seggel'

84. Hamo filius Hamonis filii Meinfelin', cujus pater obiit die Veneris ante Ascensionem, est in custodia Domini Regis, et est .xx. annorum, et habet tres sorores datas, et .j. monialem; et duxit uxorem per preceptum Domini Regis, et est de progenie comitis Warenn' ex parte patris, nepos Willelmi Mauduit ex parte matris. Terra sua in Wulrinton' valet annuatim .xxiij. *l.* cum dominio, sine placitis et tailagiis; cum hoc instauramento, scilicet, .v. carrucis, .ccc. ovibus, .x. vaccis et .j. tauro, .x. suibus et .j. verre; sed non est ibi aliquod instauramentum nisi .j. vacca.

At the foot of the roll: De Bedefordsire et Bukingh' et Roteland'. De dominabus, pueris et puellis.

[Rot. 5.]

Secundus rotulus de dominabus et puellis et pueris de Bukinghamsire, et in tergo de Roteland', demum de Huntedonsire

85. Matildis, que fuit uxor Hamonis Meinfelin', que est .xlvi. annorum, est de donatione Domini Regis. Terra sua in Stokes valet .vij. *l.* et .x. *s.*; et si esset bene instaurata, posset valere .x. *l.*

86. Filius Willelmi de Chauz, qui est .xv. annorum, est in custodia Domini Regis, et per eum in custodia Gaufridi filii Petri, elapsis .ij. annis: et terra sua in Etton' valet .ix. *l.* cum hoc instauramento, scilicet, .iij. carrucis, .ij. vaccis, .ij. suibus et .xx. ovibus; et si essent ibi quarta carruca et .iij. vacce et .j. taurus, et .iij. sues et .j. verris et .iiij.[xx.] oves, terra valeret .xj. *l.* et .x. *s.*

Seckloe Hundred

84. Hamo, son of Hamo fitz Meinfelin, whose father died the Friday before Ascension,[113] is in ward to the Lord King, is 20 years of age and has three married sisters and one who is a nun; and he married by order of the Lord King. He is from the family of the earl of Warenne on his father's side and he is a nephew of William Mauduit on his mother's.[114] His land in Wolverton is worth £23 per annum with the demesne, not counting pleas and tallages, with the following stock: viz. 5 plough-teams, 300 sheep, 10 cows, one bull, 10 sows, and one boar; but there is no stock there except for one cow.

At the foot of the roll: Concerning ladies, boys and girls of Bedfordshire, Buckinghamshire, and Rutland

[Roll 5.]

The second roll concerning ladies, girls, and boys of Buckinghamshire, and, on the dorse, concerning Rutland; finally Huntingdonshire

(Seckloe Hundred)

85. Matilda, widow of Hamo Meinfelin, is 46, and is in the Lord King's gift.[115] Her land in Stoke (Hammond) is worth £7 10s; and if it were well stocked it could be worth £10.

(Stoke Hundred)

86. The son of William de Chauz, who is 15 years of age, is in ward to the Lord King and through him has been in the wardship of Geoffrey fitz Peter for the past two years. His land in Eton is worth £9 with the following stock: viz. 3 plough-teams, 2 cows, 2 sows, and 20 sheep; and if there were a fourth plough-team, 3 cows, one bull, 3 sows, one boar, and 80 sheep the land would be worth £11 10s.[116]

---

[113] 23 May 1185; Round, *RD*, xxi. Cf. nos. 54 and 62.

[114] In other words, he was linked to the earls of Surrey and the royal chamberlain.

[115] Sister of William Mauduit, a baron and chamberlain of the Exchequer, who was also sheriff of Rutland. See nos. 84 and 96.

[116] This holding is shown by later evidence to have been part of a serjeanty by falconer service: Round, *RD*, 40, n. 1.

Hundredum de Bulenham

87. Burnham, que est terra Willelmi de Windesor', et fuit in custodia matris sue .ix. annis, valet annuatim .xx. *l.* cum hoc instauramento, scilicet, .iij. carrucis, c. ovibus, .iij. averis, .vj. suibus.

88. Chelhunte, que est terra Hamonis filii Hamonis Meinfelin', valet annuatim .x. *l.* et dim. *m.* de asiso redditu, et .viij. summis avene et dimidia.

89. Cestresham, que fuit Walteri de Bolebec, fuit jam .x. annis in custodia Reginaldi de Curten', cum filia predicti Walteri, et valet annuatim .xxx. *l.*

Hundredum de Muleshoe

90. Emme de Langetot, que est .lx. annorum, est de donatione Domini Regis, de genere illorum de Chedney'[xxiv] et Joscelini Crispini. Terra sua in Muleshoe valet .xiiij. *l.* per annum; et si apponerentur .c. oves, valeret .xv. *l.* Heredes ejus sunt uxor Alani de Dunstanuill', que est .xxx. annorum, et uxor Alardi filii Willelmi, que est .xxiiij. annorum.

91. Ida, que fuit uxor Willelmi de Schirinton', et filia Hugonis de Bulli, est de donatione Domini Regis, et est .lx. annorum, et habet .iij. filios et .iij. filias; primogenitus est .xxx. annorum. Postquam Willelmus obiit, cepit Dominus Rex terram suam in Muleshoe, et tenuit in manu sua jam .v. annis; et valet annuatim .vj. *l.* et .iij. *s.* et .vj. *d.* et .ij. anseres et .iiij. capones; et si apponerentur .ij. carruce et dimidia, et .c. oves et .v. vacce et .v. sues, valeret .x. *l.* Pars domine, que est sexta pars, valet .xxx. *s.*; et si apponeretur dimidia carruca, valeret .xl. *s.* Preter redditum, cepit vicecomes de dicta villa .lxii. *s.* et .vij. *d.*

Marginal note: Hoc est de custodiis.

[xxiv] Read "Chesney."

Burnham Hundred

87. Burnham, which is William of Windsor's land and which was in the wardship of his mother for nine years, is worth £20 per annum with the following stock: viz. 3 plough-teams, 100 sheep, 3 farm-horses, and 6 sows.[117]

88. Chalfont, which is the land of Hamo fitz Hamo Meinfelin, is worth £10 and half a mark per annum from fixed rent, and 8½ pack-loads of oats.

89. Chesham, which belonged to Walter of Bolbec, has been in the wardship of Reginald de Courtenay for 10 years, together with Walter's daughter, and it is worth £30 per annum.[118]

Moulsoe Hundred

90. Emma de Langetot, who is 60, is in the Lord King's gift, and she is from the family of Chesney and Jocelin Crispin. Her land in Moulsoe is worth £14 per annum; and if 100 sheep were placed there it would be worth £15. Her heirs are the wife of Alan of Dunstanville, who is 30, and the wife of Alard fitz William, who is 24.[119]

91. Ida, widow of William of Sherington and daughter of Hugh de Builli, is in the Lord King's gift and is 60 years old. She has three sons and three daughters; the eldest son is 30. After William died the Lord King took his land in Moulsoe (Hundred) and kept it in his possession for 5 years; and it is worth £6 3s 6d, 2 geese, and 4 capons per annum. If 2½ plough-teams, 100 sheep, 5 cows, and 5 sows were placed there the land would be worth £10. The widow's share, which is a sixth part, is worth 30s; and if half a plough-team were placed there it would be worth 40s. In addition to the rent, the sheriff took 62s 7d from the said vill.[120]

(*Marginal note*: This concerns wardships)

---

[117] According to Round, *RD*, 40, n. 2, this is an important entry for the dating of the document to 1185 rather than 1186, on the grounds that William of Windsor's death had occurred in 1175–76. See also nos. 72 and 228.

[118] See nos. 71 and 223.

[119] See nos. 99 and 135. Round, *RD*, 41, n. 1, provided this entry with the longest of footnotes, establishing in part that Emma de Langetot was the widow of Geoffrey fitz William, the greatest tenant on the Giffard fee, which was in escheat.

[120] Much about this entry is explained in A. C. Chibnall, *Sherington: Fiefs and Fields of a Buckinghamshire Village* (Cambridge, 1965), 32–35. The allocation of only one-sixth, instead of one-third, portion of the estate is considered to have been an act of reprisal by Henry II for the Sherington family's support of the young King Henry and Queen Eleanor in the revolt of 1175. It is also argued that the eldest son (Richard), aged 30, was on crusade at the time of his father's death in 1180 and remained so until 1188. He was therefore not in a position to take full possession of his inheritance.

92. Claricia, que fuit uxor Petri Morelli, est de donatione Domini Regis, et est .xlv. annorum; et habet .j. hidam et dimidiam in Crendon', de hereditate sua per servicium .j. militis ad custum Domini Regis.

Marginal note: d.

93. Filius Petri Morelli, et filius predicte Claricie, est .xv. annorum et in custodia Ricardi de Columbariis per Dominum Regem. Terra sua in Edinggraue, quam tenet de Gilberto Pipart, valet .xl. *s.* sine instauramento; et si apponerentur .j. carruca et .c. oves, valeret .iiij. *l.* Terra in Borkestall valet .x. *s.*, que est de feodo Willelmi Basset, sine instauramento; et si apponerentur dimidia carruca et .iij. sues et .j. verris, valeret .xx. *s.*

94. Filius Gileberti de Bolebec, qui est .xviij. annorum, et^{xxv} in custodia Willelmi de Charpunuill' per Dominum Regem. Terra sua in Eia valet .x. *l.*; et si apponerentur .vj. vacce, et .j. taurus, .iiij. sues, .j. verris, .lx. oves, terra valeret .xj. *l.* In eadem terra sunt .ij. domine, que sunt de donatione Domini Regis, quarum .j. est .lxx. annorum, et altera .xl. annorum, et habent duas partes dicte ville de Eia. Et Willelmus de Jarpunuill' habuit jam .v. annis tertiam partem, cum herede, et recepit preter firmam .iij. *m.*

Marginal notes: d. d.^{xxvi}

95. In villa de Burton' est quedam puella, filia Walteri de Burton', de donatione Domini Regis, et est .x. annorum; et est heres de dimidia hida terre, quam debet tenere de Rege per serianteriam despensarie: et ipsa dimidia hida valet .xij. *s.* sine instauramento, et cum instauramento valet .xix. *s.* Et puella non habet in dominio nisi .j. virgatam, aliam tenet mater ejus in dote, et quedam alia dominia.^{xxvii}

---

^{xxv} ? "est."

^{xxvi} Both notations are omitted from Round, *RD*, 43.

^{xxvii} Read "domina."

(Ixhill Hundred)

92. Clarice, widow of Peter Morel, is in the Lord King's gift and is 45 years old. She has one and a half hides in Crendon from her inheritance by service of one knight's fee at the Lord King's expense.

(*Marginal note*: d.)

93. The son of Peter Morel and of the above Clarice is 15 and in the wardship of Richard de Columbières on the Lord King's behalf. His land in Addingrove, which he holds of Gilbert Pipart, is worth 40s without stock; and if one plough-team and 100 sheep were placed there it would be worth £4. The land in Boarstall, which belongs to the fee of William Basset, is worth 10s without stock; and if half a plough-team, 3 sows, and one boar were added it would be worth 20s.

94. The son of Gilbert of Bolbec is 18 years of age and in the wardship of William de Jarpenville through the Lord King. His land in Kingsey is worth £10; and if 6 cows, one bull, 4 sows, one boar, and 60 sheep were placed there the land would be worth £11. On the same land there are two ladies who are in the Lord King's gift, one of whom is 70 and the other 40 years of age, and they have two-thirds of the said vill of Kingsey.[121] William de Jarpenville held a third part for 5 years, together with the heir, and received 3 marks as well as the farm.[122]

(*Marginal notes*: d. d.)

(Rowley Hundred)

95. In the vill of Bourton there is a girl, daughter of Walter of Bourton, in the Lord King's gift and she is 10 years of age. She is heir to half a hide of land, which she ought to hold of the Lord King by serjeanty of a steward: and this half hide is worth 12s without stock, and 19s with stock. The girl has only one virgate in demesne; her mother and a certain other lady hold the rest in dower.[123]

---

[121] There is the possibility that these two women were the mother and grandmother. See the following entry and footnote.

[122] In 1190 William de Jarpenville paid 10 marks for permission to marry his niece (*neptem*) to the heir, Herbert of Bolbec: *Pipe Roll 2 Richard I*, 145.

[123] . . . *et quedam alia dominia,* which Round suggests could be read as . . . *et quedam alia domina*: Round, *RD*, 43, n. 5. It has been suggested that the other lady was a grandmother: J. S. Loengard, " 'Of the Gift of her Husband': English Dower and its Consequences in the Year 1200," in J. Kirshner and S. F. Wemple, eds., *Women of the Medieval World* (Oxford, 1985), 215–55, here 239. See no. 75.

Hundredum de Bunestowe

96. Domina de Lateburia, que fuit uxor Johannis de Bidune et soror camerarii de Hameslepe, est in donatione Domini Regis. Terra sua in Lateburia valet .vij. *l.*; et si esset instaurata, valeret .viij. (*l.*)[xxviii]: et habet .iiij. filias maritatas; et .j. est maritanda.

Marginal note: d.[xxix]

97. Matildis Vis de Luw, que fuit filia Johannis de Bidune, est in donatione Domini Regis, et habet .ij. hidas in dote, que valent .xl. *s.*; et ipsa habet .j. filium, qui est cum Rege, et ipse est .xxij. annorum.

98. Matillis de Cremedewelle, que [fuit] filia Anfridi filii Rualdi, et uxor Ricardi Albi, est in donatione Domini Regis: et terra sua in dicta villa valet .l. *s.*, cum hoc instauramento, scilicet, .c. ovibus et .iiij. suibus et .j. verre; et ipsa est .l. annorum, et habet .ij. filios, quorum primogenitus est .xxij. annorum; et Rex reddidit ei terram suam, et preter eum habet .ix. filias.

99. Emme de Langetot habet Esinton' et Singelberge in dote, et valent .x. *l.*; et si apponerentur .c. oves, valerent .xj. *l.*; et sunt de feodo Roesie de Aubervill'.

100. Padeberia, que est terra Hamonis filii Hamonis filii Meinfelini, valet .iij. *l.* et .xij. *s.* sine dominio; et dominium valeret .iii. *l.* et .x. *s.*, si esset instauratum; et modo valet .xx. *s.*

101. Tunebrige, terra ejusdem, valet .iij. *l.* et .viij. sticas anguille[xxx] sine dominio; et si dominium esset instauratum, valeret .ij. *l.* et .v. *s.*; et modo sine instauramento valet .x. *s.*

[xxviii] Omitted from MS.
[xxix] Omitted from Round, *RD*, 43.
[xxx] Read "anguillarum."

Bunsty Hundred

96. The lady of Lathbury (Alice Mauduit), widow of John de Bidun (senior) and sister of the chamberlain from Hanslope, is in the Lord King's gift. Her land in Lathbury is worth £7, and if it were stocked it would be worth £8. She has four married daughters and one yet to be married.[124]

(*Marginal note*: d.)

97. Matilda Vis-de-Loup, daughter of John de Bidun, is in the Lord King's gift and has two hides in dower, which are worth 40s. She has one son, who is with the Lord King, and he is 22.[125]

98. Matilda of Cranwell, daughter of Amfrid fitz Ruald and widow of Richard Albus, is in the Lord King's gift. Her land in the said vill is worth 50s with the following stock: viz. 100 sheep, 4 sows, and one boar; and she is 50 years of age and has two sons, of whom the elder is 22; and the Lord King returned his land to him, and besides him she has nine daughters.

99. Emma de Langetot holds Easington and Singleborough[126] in dower and they are worth £10; and if 100 sheep were placed there they would be worth £11. They belong to the fee of Rose of Auberville.

(Lamua Hundred)

100. Padbury, the land of Hamo son of Hamo fitz Meinfelin, is worth £3 12s without the demesne; and the demesne would be worth £3 10s if it were stocked; and currently it is worth 20s.

101. Thornborough, the land of the same man, is worth £3 and 8 sticks of eels,[127] not counting the demesne; and if the demesne were stocked it would be worth £2 5s; and now without stock it is worth 10s.

---

[124] See no. 104, where the marriages are listed.

[125] As Round, *RD*, 44, n. 1, puts it: "The age of the son . . . raises a difficulty," but it is not as great as that of the 60-year-old William of Lanvaley in entry no. 201 or the 30-year-old son in no. 91. The land is unidentified.

[126] Easington is in Ixhill Hundred and Singleborough in Mursley Hundred.

[127] I.e. 160–200 eels. The measure of a 'stick' probably derives from the practice of carrying a number of eels, generally 20 to 25, on a stick passed through the gills. See H. C. Darby, *Domesday Geography* (Cambridge, 1977), 279.

102. Matillis, que fuit filia Roberti de Riblemunt, habet in Bukingham .xx. acras terre in .j. campo, et .xx. in alio, cum prato quod adjacet terre; et est de donatione Domini Regis, et est .lxxx. annorum, et nullum habet heredem. Et defendit terram suam per serianteriam eundi in servitio Regis infra Angliam ad custum suum, et ultra mare ad custum Domini Regis; et tota terra valet .xvj. *s.*, et non potest plus valere.

[Rot. 5. d.]

Rotulus de dominabus et puellis et pueris de Roteland'

103. Roeis de Bussey, que fuit filia Baldewini filii Gileberti, est in donatione Domini Regis, et est .lx. annorum. Terra sua in Issendene valet .x. *l.* cum hoc instauramento, scilicet, .iiij. carrucis, .c. ovibus, sed desunt .c. oves. Ipsa cepit .x. *m.* de bosco suo infra hos .viij. annos, et .xx. *s.* de placea. Ipsa habet .ij. filias heredes: altera est uxor Hugonis Wak, altera Johannis de Bulli.

104. Aliz de Bidune, soror Willelmi Mauduit, est de donatione Domini Regis, et est .l. annorum. Terra sua in Morcote, cum pertinenciis, valet per annum .x. *l.*, cum .j. carruca que ibi est. Ipsa habet .iiij. filias: primogenitam habet Hugo de Clint' per Dominum Regem, secundam Milo de Bellocampo, tertiam Ricardus de Bellocampo, quartam Gaufridus filius Gaufridi. Preter firmam cepit de terra sua post mortem mariti sui de auxilio .xxiiij. *s.*

105. Aliz de Beaufow, que fuit uxor Thome de Beaufow, est in donatione Domini Regis, que fuit filia Walerani de Orri et neptis Alexandri filii Nigelli, est .xx. annorum, et habet .j. filium heredem, qui est .ij. annorum. Terra sua in Seiton'

(Rowley Hundred)

102. Matilda, daughter of Robert de Riblemont, has 20 acres of land in one field in Buckingham and 20 in another, with meadow belonging to the land; and she is in the Lord King's gift. She is 80 years old and has no heir. She holds her land by serjeanty of travelling in the Lord King's service within England at her own expense, and overseas at the Lord King's expense. The whole land is worth 16s, and it cannot be worth more.[128]

[Roll 5. dorse.]

Roll concerning ladies, boys and girls of Rutland

(Witchley Hundred)

103. Rose de Bussy, daughter of Baldwin fitz Gilbert (de Clare), is in the Lord King's gift and is 60. Her land in Essendine is worth £10 (per annum) with the following stock: viz. 3 plough-teams and 100 sheep, but the 100 sheep are not there. She herself took 10 marks from her wood in this period of eight years,[129] and 20s from a plot of land. She has two daughters as heirs; one is married to Hugh Wake, the other to John de Builli.[130]

104. Alice de Bidun, sister of William Mauduit, is in the Lord King's gift and is 50. Her land in Morcott with its appurtenances is worth £10 per annum with one plough-team, which is there. She has four daughters: the eldest is married to Hugh de Clinton through the Lord King, the second to Miles de Beauchamp, the third to Richard de Beauchamp, the fourth to Geoffrey fitz Geoffrey. Apart from the farm she took 24s in aid from her land after her husband's death.[131]

105. Alice de Belfou, widow of Thomas de Belfou, is in the Lord King's gift. She was a daughter of Waleran d'Oiri and niece of Nigel fitz Alexander.[132] She is 20 years old and has one son and heir, who is two years old. Her land in Seaton is

---

[128] This was a minor serjeanty, which seems to have disappeared at an early date. It does not appear in Round, *The King's Serjeants*.

[129] This seems to be the force of *infra hos .viii. annos*, as opposed to annual returns.

[130] In no. 22 Rose, aged 50, appears as the widow of William de Bussy.

[131] See no. 96. Round, *RD*, xliii, identifies the four daughters as Amice, Mabel, Sarah, and Matilda.

[132] Sheriff of Lincolnshire. Corrected by Round, *RD*, 45–46, n. 3, from Alexander fitz Nigel. The correct name is given in nos. 49, 140, and 141.

valet annuatim .viij. *m.*, cum hoc instauramento, scilicet, .ij. carrucis, .c. ovibus, .ij. averis, .v. suibus, .j. verre, et .iiij. vaccis. De firma terre sue recepit ipsa hoc primo anno quo fuit terra in manu sua .xxxvj. *s.* et. .x. *d.* et .ij. libras piperis; et preter firmam dederunt ei homines .iiij. *s.*, et .iij. summas avene.

Rotulus de dominabus et pueris de Huntedun'sire et puellis

Hundredum de Leitonested'

106. Kenebolton', que fuit de feodo Willelmi de Say, fuit in manu Domini Regis cum filiabus predicti Willelmi, et in custodia Ricardi Rufi per .vij. annos. Et preterea ab Augusto usque ad festum Omnium Sanctorum,[xxxi] et interim, recepit predictus Ricardus de predicta villa de asiso redditu .lv. *l.* et .xv. *s.* et xj. *d.*; et de auxilio .iiij.[xx.] *l.*[xxxii] et iiij. *l.*, et .xiii. *s.* et .iiij. *d.*; et de forefactis, .lxj. [*l.*] et .iiij. *s.* et .ix. *d.*; et de franccis (*sic*) hominibus pro exitibus et fine placitorum, .xxiij. *l.* et .xij. *s.* et .viij. *d.*; et de nemore quod vocatur La Haie .xv. *l.*; et de .j. vaccaria .x. *s.*, de orreis .c. et .xxx. *l.* Preterea ipse Ricardus duxit de curia dicte ville .xx. boves et .v. vaccas et .iij. averos. Preterea de predicta [La] Haia cepit ipse .cc. et .xxij. quercus, quarum .xlij. dedit ubi voluit, et de aliis fecit sibi fieri aulam et cameram in Leicestresire, et de .lxxx. fasciculis virgarum, quos cepit de predicto nemore. Quando ipse cepit villam, ipsa valuit annuatim .xxxij. *l.*, et modo valet .xl. *l.*, cum instauramento .viij. carrucarum, qualibet de .viij. bobus, et .ccc. ovibus, .x. ovibus, .j. tauro.

107. Clemencia de Sancto Claro est in donatione Domini Regis, et est .lx. annorum; et ipsa tenet Haut' de Willelmo de Lanualei, que valet annuatim xx .*l.*, cum instauramento .iiij. carrucarum et .ccc. ovibus.

[xxxi] Round, *RD*, 46, n. 1, argues that the words "Et preterea . . . Sanctorum" should be read with the previous sentence.

[xxxii] Round, *RD*, 46: ".iii.[xx.] l."

worth 8 marks per annum with the following stock: viz. 2 plough-teams, 100 sheep, 2 farm-horses, 5 sows, one boar, and 4 cows. In the first year that it was in her possession she received 36s 10d and 2 pounds of pepper from the farm of her land. And in addition to the farm the men (of the vill) gave her 4s and 3 pack-loads of oats.

Roll concerning ladies, boys, and girls of Huntingdonshire

Leightonstone Hundred

106. Kimbolton, which belongs to the fee of William de Say, was in the Lord King's possession, together with the (two) daughters of the said William,[133] and it was in the wardship of Richard Rufus for seven years, as well as from August to the feast of All Saints (1 November). In this period Richard received £55 15s 11d in fixed rent from the said vill, £84 13s 4d from aids, £61 4s 9d from forfeitures, £23 12s 8d from the freemen for the issue and settlement of pleas, £15 from the wood which is called La Haye, 10s from the vaccary, and £130 from the barns.[134] Furthermore, the same Richard took 20 oxen, 5 cows, and 3 farm-horses from the courtyard of the said vill. He also took 222 oaks from the above Haye, of which he gave (away) 42 where he wished, and from the others and 80 bundles of withies, which he took from the same wood, he had a hall and chamber built for himself in Leicestershire. When he took over the vill it was worth £32 per annum, and now it is worth £40, with stock of 8 plough-teams, each of 8 oxen, 310 sheep, and one bull.[135]

107. Clemence of Saint Clair is in the Lord King's gift and is 60 years of age. She holds *Haut*'[136] of William de Lanvaley, which is worth £20 per annum, with stock of 4 plough-teams and 300 sheep.

---

[133] The number of daughters is provided by no. 115. Their names were Beatrice and Matilda. Beatrice married Geoffrey fitz Peter, who through his wife's connection with the Mandeville family claimed that honour on William de Mandeville's death in 1189. William de Say had died in 1177. See R. V. Turner, "The Mandeville Inheritance, 1189–1236: Its Legal, Political and Social Context," *Haskins Society Journal* 1 (1989): 147–72.

[134] Round, *RD*, xxviii, has £84 13s 4d from aids (which is correct) and £61 4s 9d from forfeitures. Round's printed text gives £64 13s 4d from aids. In the case of forfeitures it is very likely that the £ has been omitted from *.lxj.[l.] et .iiij. s. et .ix. d.* The sums are so large that it seems that the meaning of *interim* must be the whole of the period that the estate was in Richard Rufus's hand. Cf. no. 115.

[135] Although, therefore, the custodian seems to have fully, perhaps more than fully, exploited the estate, it seems to have been left in a more prosperous condition. Cf. no. 38.

[136] Possibly Houghton in Hurstingstone Hundred. See also no. 169, where Clemence, widow of Hubert of Saint Clair, appears as 80 years of age.

[Rot. 6.]

Rotulus de dominabus, pueris et puellis de Norfolk'

108. Alicia de Hemeford' tenet Hemeford' in dote de dono Gileberti Blundi; et modo valet .viij. *l.*, et cum instauramento .j. carruce et .c. ovium posset valere .x. *l.* Ipsa fuit filia Ricardi de Colechirche, et est .xl. annorum, et tenet Hemeford' de Huberto filio suo, qui est in custodia episcopi Eliensis, et est .xx. annorum.

109. Agnes de Mundeuill' tenet Heilesdune et habet custodiam filiorum[xxxiii] suorum per Dominum Regem; et Heilesdune est de feodo Humfridi de Buhun, et valet modo .xviij. *l.*, et cum instauramento .cc. ovium, que possent ibi esse, villa valeret .xx. *l.* Et ipsa est .l. annorum, et fuit filia Roberti Gresley, et habet .iiij. filios de Teodbaldo Hautein, et primogenitus est .xv. annorum.

110. Cecilia de Buutorp est de donatione Domini Regis, que .ij. viros habuit, scilicet, Hugonem de Scotcia (*sic*) et Ewstachium de Leiham. De Hugone .iij. filios habuit, et de Ewstacio .ij. filios et .ii. filias. Reginaldus, filius suus primogenitus et heres, est .xxiiij. annorum, cujus pater Ewstacius fuit de parentela comitis de Meuland', et consanguineus Roberti filii Humfridi. Predicta Cecilia est de parentela comitis de Reduers, et est .l. annorum. Ejus terra in Buutorp valet cum rationabili instauramento .viij. *l.* In eadem villa Rogerus de Ho tenet quartam partem feodi .j. militis de eadem Cecilia, preter illas .viij. *l.* Predictus Reginaldus, filius suus, uxorem habet, scilicet, neptem vicecomitis Wimeri, quam, ut Wimer dicit, per Dominum Regem habuit.

[xxxiii] Corrected from "filiam" in MS.

[Roll 6.]

Roll concerning ladies, boys, and girls of Norfolk

(Taverham Hundred)

108. Alice of Hainford holds Hainford in dower as the gift of Gilbert Blund; and currently it is worth £8, and with stock of one plough-team and 100 sheep it could be worth £10.[137] She herself was the daughter of Richard of Colkirk and is 40 years of age, and she holds Hainford of Hubert, her son, who is 20 years of age and in the wardship of the bishop of Ely.[138]

109. Agnes of Amundeville holds Hellesdon and has wardship of her sons through the Lord King; and Hellesdon belongs to the fee of Humphrey de Bohun and it is worth £18 at present, and with stock of 200 sheep, which could be there, the vill would be worth £20. And she herself is 50 years of age and was the daughter of Robert Grelley. She has three sons of Theobald Hautein and the eldest is 15 years of age.[139]

(Forehoe Hundred)

110. Cecilia of Bowthorpe is in the Lord King's gift, and she has had two husbands, Hugh of Scotland and Eustace of Leyham. She had three sons by Hugh, and two sons and two daughters by Eustace. Reginald, her eldest son and heir, is 24 years of age, and his father, Eustace, belonged to the count of Meulan's family and was a kinsman of Robert fitz Humphrey. The aforesaid Cecilia is from the family of the earl de Redvers and is 50 years of age. Her land in Bowthorpe is worth £8 with reasonable stock. In the same vill Roger de Hoo holds a quarter of a knight's fee of the same Cecilia, as well as the £8. The above Reginald, her son, married a niece of the sheriff Wimer, and according to Wimer, he married her with the Lord King's permission.

---

[137] As with no. 93, one plough-team and 100 sheep were worth £2 to the estate.

[138] For two later entries concerning Hubert, son of William Blund, not Gilbert Blund. See nos. 162–163.

[139] See no. 130, where Agnes is recorded as 40 and her eldest son as 14. *Pipe Roll 31 Henry II*, 34, records Agnes accounting for £12 1s 8d for the wardship of her sons and their land.

111. Filius Alberti Gresley est in custodia Domini Regis, et nunc est cum Gil-leberto Basset, avunculo suo, per Dominum Regem, et est .xj. annorum. Villa de Tunstede, que fuit predicti Alberti, est in custodia Nigelli filii Alexandri et Roberti de Burrun, qui additis .c. ovibus accreverunt firmam ville de .xx. *s.*; et est villa ad firmam pro .xx. *l.*, nec posset amplius extendi. Dicta villa fuit in manu Domini Regis jam per .v. annos, et a festo Sancti Michaelis usque ad Purifica-tionem in custo[dia] Thome Basset; postea in custodia predictorum. Primis .ij. annis, reddidit terra de Tunstede .xix. *l.*; postea annuatim .xx. *l.* Dictus Albertus habuit .j. filium et .iij. filias.

112. Uxor que fuit Ricardi la Ueile, qui obiit ad festum Sancti Michaelis, est in donatione Domini Regis, et fuit filia Amfridi Buteturte, et est .xxx. annorum. Terra sua in Haniges, quam habet in dote, est de feodo Willelmi de Edesfeld', et valet annuatim .vij. *l.* Ricardus, heres predicti Ricardi Laueile, est .vj. anno-rum, et in custodia matris et avunculorum suorum (*sic*), scilicet, Thome Basset, per Dominum Regem, sicut vicecomes et juratores testantur. Terra Ricardi filii predicti Ricardi in Witon', valet annuatim .lx. *s.*, et (*sic*) de serianteria Domini Regis.

113. Filius Roberti filii Radulfi, qui obiit ad festum Sancte Crucis, est in custodia Domini Regis, et est nepos Rannulfi de Glanuill', et adhuc cum eo, et est .xv. annorum. Villa sua de Herdeseta est de feodo comitis Britannie, et valet annuatim .xxij. *l.* et .xiiij. *s.* cum hoc instauramento, scilicet, .iij. carrucis et .vj. vaccis et .vj. suibus; et hoc ibi est, et plus pati non potest.

(Tunstead Hundred)

111. The son of Albert Grelley is in ward to the Lord King and is now with Gilbert Basset, his uncle, through the Lord King, and he is 11 years of age. The vill of Tunstead, which belonged to Albert Grelley, is in the wardship of Nigel fitz Alexander and Robert de Burun, who, with the addition of 100 sheep, increased the farm of the vill by 20s;[140] and the vill is at farm for £20 and it could not be increased further. The said vill was in the Lord King's hand for 5 years, and from Michaelmas to the Purification (2 February) in the wardship of Thomas Basset;[141] and afterwards in the wardship of the aforesaid men (Nigel fitz Alexander and Robert de Burun); in the first two years the land of Tunstead rendered £19, afterwards £20 per annum. Albert had one son and three daughters.

112. The widow of Richard la Veile, who died at Michaelmas, is in the Lord King's gift. She was a daughter of Amfrid Buteturte and is 30 years of age. Her land in Honing, which she has in dower, belongs to the fee of William of Edgefield, and is worth £7 per annum. Richard, the heir of Richard la Veile, is 6 years of age and is in the wardship of his mother and his uncles (*sic*), viz. Thomas Basset, through the Lord King, according to the testimony of the sheriff and the jurors. The land of Richard, son of the said Richard, in Witton is worth 60s per annum, and belongs to a serjeanty of the Lord King.[142]

(Humbleyard Hundred)

113. The son of Robert fitz Ralph, who died at the feast of the Holy Cross,[143] is in ward to the Lord King, and he is a nephew of Rannulf Glanvill, and is still with him;[144] he is 15 years old. His vill of Hethersett belongs to the fee of the count of Brittany, and is worth £22 14s per annum with the following stock: viz. 3 plough-teams, 6 cows, and 6 sows; and they are there, and it is not possible to sustain more.

---

[140] As in no. 71, the heir and the property appear to be in different hands.

[141] 29 September 1184–2 February 1185.

[142] In no. 129 the heir appears (rightly, according to Round, *RD*, 49, n. 1; and 54, n. 4) as Roger, son of Richard la Veile. The serjeanty was for goshawk service.

[143] The feast of the Holy Cross is 14 September.

[144] Presumably in the wardship of Rannulf Glanvill.

114. Uxor que fuit Johannis de Bidune junioris, Matillis nomine, est in donatione Domini Regis, et est .x. annorum, et fuit filia Thome filii Bernardi. Terra sua in Kirkebi valet .vj. *l.*, cum instauramento .j. carruce, et non potest plus valere.

115. Due filie Willelmi de Say fuerunt in custodia Domini Regis, cum Suham que fuit terra ejus Willelmi, et per Dominum Regem in custodia Ricardi Ruffi .vij. annis, et tanto tempore quantum est inter festum Sancti Petri ad Vincula et .xv. dies post festum Sancti Michaelis; postea recepit Galfridus filius Petri Suham, cum filia Willelmi de Say. Firma de Suham sunt annuatim .xxiij. *l.* et .xvj. *s.* et .viij. *d.*, et quinquies[xxxiv] .xx., et .xviij. summe de brasio et .xxiiij. summe de sale et .x. arietes. Hanc firmam recepit Ricardus Ruffus .vii. annis, et in octavo anno ad unum terminum .vj. *l.* et .ij. *s.* et .j. *d.* Preter firmam recepit Ricardus Ruffus infra predictum terminum de soka de Suham .iiij.^{c} *m.* de auxilio et de placitis .xxiij. *l.* et .iij. *s.*, de herieti (*sic*) hominum .ix. *l.* et .xvij. *s.*,[xxxv] de gersumis .iij. *l.* et .iij. *s.* et .ii. *d.*, de Ernaldo de Meisy .ij. *m.*, de exitu orreorum infra predictum terminum .xxxiiij. *l.* et .xj. *s.* et .xj. *d.* Hoc instauramentum recepit Ricardus in

---

[xxxiv] MS: ".v.^{es}xx." The superscript is immediately above ".v." Grimaldi reads "verres xx."

[xxxv] Round, *RD*, 50: "de herietis hominum .ix. *l.* et .xvii. *s.*" There is a strong suggestion that the ".ix. *l.*" should read ".xx. *l.*"

(Henstead Hundred)

114. Matilda, widow of John de Bidun Junior, is in the Lord King's gift and is 10 years of age, and she was a daughter of Thomas fitz Bernard.[145] Her land in Kirby is worth £6 with stock of one plough-team, and it cannot be worth more.[146]

(Wayland Hundred)

115. The two daughters of William de Say were in ward to the Lord King,[147] together with Saham, which was William's land, and through the Lord King they were in the wardship of Richard Rufus for seven years and for the period from the feast of Saint Peter ad Vincula to fifteen days after Michaelmas.[148] Afterwards Geoffrey fitz Peter took possession of Saham, as well as marrying one of the daughters of William de Say.[149] The annual farm of Saham is worth £23 16s 8d[150] and 118 pack-loads of malt, 24 seams of salt, and 10 rams. Richard Rufus received this farm for seven years, and in the eighth year (he received) £6 2s 1d for the one term. Besides the farm, within the aforesaid term (of seven years?) Richard Rufus took 400 marks[151] in aid from the soke of Saham, £23 3s from pleas, £20 17s from the men's heriot dues, £3 3s 2d from marriage fines, 2 marks from Ernald de Meisy, and £34 11s 11d from the proceeds of the barns within the aforesesaid term.[152] Richard received the following stock in the manor of Saham:

---

[145] The royal master forester.

[146] Widowhood at the age of 10 was abnormal, even in the Middle Ages. See no. 227, which refers to Matilda's marriage, but not her widowhood.

[147] Normally widows and heiresses were said to be in the King's gift, rather than in wardship (see Introduction). Two other examples of a widow and an heiress in wardship occur in nos. 154 and 179.

[148] From 1 August to 13 October.

[149] The elder daughter, Beatrice. See entry no. 106. Geoffrey fitz Peter succeeded Thomas fitz Bernard as master forester of England, and became justiciar in 1198. He was also the custodian in nos. 60 and 86.

[150] Round, *RD*, xxviii, has £23 6s 8d., and introduces 20 boars as part of the farm. Admittedly the text is difficult at this point. Round has interpreted *V.es .xx.* in the MS as *verres .xx.*, whereas in the text (following Grimaldi) it is extended to *quinquies .xx.*, which would be an unusual way of indicating 100, to add to the 18 pack-loads of malt grain. However, nowhere else in the MS is *verres* abbreviated in this way. In the MS the superscipt "es" is placed immediately above the "v."

[151] The MS has *de soka de Suham .iiii.ᶜ m.* (or possibly *.iiii.ᵗ· m.*). Round, *RD*, xxviii, translates as 4 marks from the soke of the manor.

[152] The totals begin and end with the expression *infra predictum terminum*. The amounts suggest the whole term of Richard Rufus's custodianship, as in no. 106.

predicto manerio de Suham: .xxx. boves et .x. averos et .j. vaccam et .xl. oves et .xiiij. sues; et quando restituit manerium Galfrido remanserunt in Suham .xiiij. boves et .viij. averi.

116. Agnes de Muntchenesy est in donatione Domini Regis, et est .lx. annorum, que [fuit] filia Pagani filii Johannis, et habet .iij. filios: primogenitus vocatur Radulfus, et secundus Willelmus, qui ambo sunt milites; tertius vocatur Hubertus, et est clericus. Ipsa habet .ij. filias, quarum una est nupta Stephano de Gla[n]uill', et altera Willelmo Painel. Ipsa habet in Holkham .xj. libratas terre, ...[xxxvi] sine instauramento, et terra sua in Holkham posset pati de instauramento .j. carrucam et .c. oves et tunc valeret .xiij. *l.* Ista terra est de feodo comitis Sudsex', et dicta domina tenet de Radulfo filio suo.

117. Ade de Tony est in donatione Domini Regis, et est .xxx. annorum, et fuit [filia] Roberti de Chaumunt, et .j. filium [habet], B[aldewinum] nomine, qui est .xv. annorum, et ipsa habet .v. filias. Et in Holkham habet ipsa .c. solidatas terre, quas tenet de feodo Rogeri de Tony, et plus non potest valere. Et ipsa tenet de Baldewino filio suo.

118. Amicia de Limesia est in donatione Domini Regis, et est .lx. annorum, que fuit filia Hanelað[xxxvii] de Bid[une et habet] .ii. filios milites, quorum primogenitus vocatur Johannes de Limesia; plures habet filias. Ipsa habet in . . . . xl. solidatas terre de feodo Johannis de Limesia; et de eo tenet.

119. Middelt' cum pertinenciis cecidit in manum Domini Regis post mortem Comitis Walteri Giffard', quam villam Willelmus [de] Gernemuwe tenuit de comite pro .xx. *l.,* et postea de Rege, qui tandem remisit ei .iiij. *s.* [an]nuatim pro servitio suo.[xxxviii] Post mortem Willelmi, qui obiit elapsis .iiij. annis et dimidio,

---

[xxxvi] This section is illegible even with ultra-violet lamp treatment. The right-hand side of the MS is very damaged to the end of the membrane.

[xxxvii] Here and in entry no. 126 there is a very late use of the Anglo-Saxon thorn.

[xxxviii] The MS has no punctuation here, but, as Round pointed out, it makes more sense to begin the next sentence with "Post mortem Willelmi": Round, *RD,* 51, n. 4.

30 oxen, 10 farm-horses, one cow, 40 sheep, and 14 sows. When he restored the manor to Geoffrey there remained 14 oxen and 8 farm-horses.[153]

(North Greenhoe Hundred)

116. Agnes de Mountchesney is in the Lord King's gift and is 60 years of age; she was a daughter of Payn fitz John and has three sons. The eldest is called Ralph, the second William, and they are both knights. The third is called Hubert and he is a clerk. She has two daughters, of whom one was married to Stephen Glanvill, and the other to William Paynel. She herself has 11 librates of land in Holkham, . . . without stock, and her land in Holkham could sustain stock of one plough-team and 100 sheep, and then it would be worth £13. The land belongs to the fee of the earl of Sussex,[154] and the above lady holds it of her son, Ralph.

117. Ada de Toeni is in the Lord King's gift and is 30. She was the daughter of Robert de Chaumunt and has one son, Baldwin by name, who is 15, and five daughters. She has 100 solidates of land in Holkham, which she holds of the fee of Roger de Toeni, and it cannot be worth more. She holds of her son Baldwin.

(South Greenhoe Hundred)

118. Amice de Limesy is in the Lord King's gift and is 60 years of age. She was the daughter of Haldenald de Bidun and has two sons, who are knights, of whom the elder is called John de Limesy; she has several daughters. She has in . . .[155] 40 solidates of land of the fee of John de Limesy and holds it of him.

119. Middleton with its appurtenances fell into the Lord King's hand after the death of Earl Walter Giffard.[156] William of Yarmouth held this vill of the earl for £20, and afterwards of the Lord King, who finally remitted 4s per annum to him for his service.[157] After the death of William, who died four and a half

---

[153] By contrast with no. 106, there seems to have been a serious depletion of this estate of William de Say.

[155] William d'Aubigny.

[156] MS. torn. Round, *RD*, 51, n. 3, suggests that her dower would have been in Oxborough or Didlington in South Greenhoe Hundred, the Domesday manors of her husband's family.

[156] Earl Giffard died in 1164 without male heirs. The barony escheated to the Crown and remained in the king's hand until the early years of Richard I, when it was divided between the Clares and the Marshals: Sanders, *English Baronies*, 62. There is a Middleton in Depwade Hundred and another in Freebridge Hundred.

[157] The pipe roll account for this year indicates that this should be a remission of £4, not 4s: *Pipe Roll 30 Henry II*, 13.

Dominus Rex tra[didit] custodiam . . . . . .puerorum predicti Willelmi et custodiam predicte terre Radulfo de Hauuill' pro .xvj. *l* . . . . et valet annuatim .xx. *l.*, cum .xij. bobus et .j. caballo hercerio. Et si .c. o[ves], ... et .v. vacce, et .v. sues et .x. juvenes porci, cum .j. porco .j. anni ibi a[pponerentur,] valeret .xxj. *l.* et dim. Predictus Willelmus, dum tenuit intra hos .viij. annos r[ecepit?] de placitis et fortunis et .xij. *s.* et .viij. *d.*, et .j. *m.* de gersumis fem[inarum] et .v. *s.* et .x. *d.* de releviis liberorum hominum.

120. Willelmus de Gernemue tenuit quoddam [l]estagium^{xxxix} de Domino Rege pro .vj. *l.*, et Radulfus de Hauuill' tenet [custodiam?] puerorum, et tempore Henrici Regis avi Domini Regis solet esse ad firmam pro .x. *l* . . . . runt propter [l]estagium de Dunewich', et istud [l]estagium colligitur in .iij. comitatibus, scilicet . . . . . . [Lin]colsire. Item Radulfus de Hauuill' recipit de predicta custodia in Lenna .iiij. *m* . . . . xvj. gallinas et .iiij. altilia, de feodo episcopi Norwicensis et aliorum dominorum. Willelmus [de Gernemue habuit] .iij. filios, quorum primogenitus est .xxij. annorum, secundus .xviij., tertius .xv., et sunt . . . . . .

121. Filius Petri de Peleuill', qui obiit .xv. diebus ante proximum festum Omnium Sanctorum, est in custodia Domini Regis . . . . . . et habet fratrem qui nondum est .j. anni, et duas sorores que sunt cum matre sua, que est de . . . . . . annorum. In Bodeneia habuit dictus Petrus terram que est dos uxoris sue, de Constab . . . . . . de dote sua, .x. *s.* de redditu ad Pascha. Hec terra valet .c. *s.* cum instaura[mento] . . . . . . bobus et .iiij. equis et .vj. vaccis et .viij. animalibus otiosis et .v. porcis; et si alia car[ruca apponeretur], terra valeret .viij. *l.*

[Rot. 6. d.]

122. Beleneia, que est de honore de Hagenet, est in manu Domini Regis cum heredibus Petri de Peleuill', a festo Sancti Thome Apostoli. Predictus Petrus habuit .ij. filios; et primogenitus est .xxiiij. annorum, et est leprosus, et est in

---

^{xxxix} Round, *RD*, 52, n. 2, corrects to "lestagium."

years ago, the Lord King handed over wardship of the sons of the said William and the above land to Ralph de Hauville for £16 . . . (per annum?) . . . and it is worth £20 per annum with 12 oxen, and one horse for harrowing. And if 100 sheep . . ., 5 cows, 5 sows, 10 young pigs, and one yearling pig were added it would be worth £21 10s. The aforesaid William, while he was in possession for these eight years . . . (received?) . . . from pleas and profits 12s 8d and one mark from marriage fines . . . and 5s 10d from the reliefs of freemen.

120. William of Yarmouth held a certain lastage[158] of the Lord King for £6 and Ralph de Hauville has . . . (wardship?) . . . of the sons, and in the time of King Henry, grandfather of the Lord King, it was accustomed to be at farm for £10 . . . on account of the lastage of Dunwich,[159] and that lastage is collected in 3 counties, viz. . . . (Norfolk, Suffolk and?) . . . Lincolnshire. Also Ralph de Hauville received from the said wardship 4 marks in (King's) Lynn . . . 16 hens and 4 capons from the fee of the bishop of Norwich and from other lords. William of Yarmouth had three sons, of whom the eldest is 22, the second 18, the third 15, and they are . . .

(South Greenhoe Hundred)

121. The son of Peter de Pelleville, who died 15 days before the feast of All Saints last past,[160] is in ward to the Lord King . . . and he has a brother not yet one year old and two sisters who are with their mother, who is (46) years old.[161] In Bodney the said Peter held land, which is his wife's dower, of Constab . . . from her dower 10s in rent at Easter. This land is worth 100s with stock (of) . . . oxen, 3 horses, 6 cows, 8 non-working beasts, and 5 pigs, and if another plough-team were added the land would be worth £8.

[Roll 6. dorse]

(Freebridge Hundred)

122. Bilney, which belongs to the honour of Haughley, is in the Lord King's hand with the heirs of Peter de Pelleville from the feast of Saint Thomas the Apostle.[162] The said Peter had two sons: the firstborn is 24 and a leper. He is in

---

[158] The right to farm export duty.

[159] Co. Suffolk.

[160] This would be 16 October, not 16 November, as in Round, *RD*, 52–53, n. 3. The heir's leprosy (see next entry) kept his land in the King's hand.

[161] Evidence for her age is provided by no. 123.

[162] 21 December 1184. The honour of Haughley escheated to the crown in 1163: Sanders, *English Baronies*, 121.

custodia Domini Regis, et habet sustentationem in hospitio. Secundus nondum est .j. anni. Preterea dictus Petrus habuit .ij. filias maritandas; primogenita est .xiiij. annorum, secunda .v. annorum. Robertus de Well' et Willelmus de Essedeford' receperunt custodiam ad festum Sancti Thome Apostoli, qui de omnibus exitibus, scilicet, de redditibus et perquisitis, receperunt .iiij. *l.* et viij. *s.* et .vij. *d.* Et hoc manerium valet .x. *l.* cum instauramento quod ibi est, scilicet, .j. carruca de .vj. bobus et .ij. equis, et .viij. vaccis et .lxvj. ovibus inter oves et agnos, et .xviij. porcis. Et cum pleno instauramento, scilicet, .iiij. carrucis, qualibet de .vj. bobus et .ij. equis, et .j. hercerio et .xx. vaccis et .ccc. ovibus et .xxx. porcis, villa valeret .xvj. *l.* post hunc annum: et precipitur instaurari.

123. Uxor Petri de Peleuill' est in donatione Domini Regis, et est .xlvj. annorum, et nata de militibus, et habet Bodeneiam in dote.

124. Beatricia de Saiton' tenet feodum dimidii militis de eschaeta Walteri Giffard', et est heritagium suum, et valet per annum .xl. *s.* Ipsa est .l. annorum, et habet .vj. filios, et .j. filiam maritandam: primogenitus est .xxj. anni, et sunt nati de militibus.

125. Maria, uxor Gwidonis Extraney, est in donatione Domini Regis, et habet in dote Runget' de feodo de Wermegai; valet villa annuatim .xiiij. *l.* Ipsa est .xl. annorum et nata de militibus et baronibus. Habuit ipsa .iij. dominos. Dotes ejus et maritagium sunt in diversis comitatibus.

Hundredum de Crauering'

126. Agnes de Muntchenesy habet in hundredo de Crauering, Bergche, que valet annuatim .xx. *l.*, et est de feodo Sancte Ethelðrede.

the Lord King's wardship, and has a living in a hospice. The second is not yet one year old. Furthermore the said Peter had two daughters as yet unmarried: the elder one is 14 years of age, the younger is 5. Robert of Wells and William of Ashford took wardship at the feast of Saint Thomas the Apostle, and they received from all sources, that is from rents and perquisites (of court), £4 8s 7d. This manor is worth £10 with the existing stock, namely one plough-team of 6 oxen and 2 horses, 8 cows, 66 sheep, taking sheep and lambs together, and 18 pigs. And with full stock, viz. 3 plough-teams, each with 6 oxen and 2 horses, one harrow-beast, 20 cows, 300 sheep, and 30 pigs, the vill would be worth £16 after this year. It was ordered to be stocked.[163]

(South Greenhoe Hundred)

123. The widow of Peter de Pelleville is in the Lord King's gift, is 46 years old, born of the knightly class and has Bodney in dower.[164]

124. Beatrice de Saiton has a half knight's fee from the escheat of Walter Giffard.[165] It is her inheritance and is worth 40s per annum. She is 50 and has six sons and one daughter yet to be married. The eldest son is 21. They (the children) were born of knights.[166]

(Clackclose Hundred)

125. Mary, wife of Guy l'Estrange, is in the Lord King's gift and has in dower Runcton of the fee of Wormegay. The vill is worth £14 per annum. She is 40 and born of knights and barons. She has had three husbands. Her dowers and marriage portion are in various counties.

Clavering Hundred

126. Agnes de Mountchesney has Burgh in Clavering Hundred and it is worth £20 per annum and belongs to the fee of Saint Etheldreda.[167]

---

[163] It is notable that manor and vill are used interchangeably in this entry. Likewise in entry no. 162.

[164] Her dower in Bodney is described in no. 121.

[165] See no. 119.

[166] Holding unidentified.

[167] I.e. the bishopric of Ely.

Hundredum de Happinges

127. Agnes de Muntchenesy tenet in hundredo de Happinges .xvj. libratas terre in Sutton' de feodo Rogeri le Bigot.

128. Ricardus de Coleka tenuit villam de Hemested' in eodem hundredo, que est feodum dimidii militis, et tenebat in capite de Domino Rege, et mortuus est. Et Gaufridus Pecche cepit uxorem suam per Hugonem de Cressi: et quedam neptis predicti Ricardi remansit heres ejus inde, et Rogerus de [Sancto] Di[o]nosio (*sic*)[xl] cepit eam in uxorem per Hugonem de Cressi, et ita habet terram illam, que valet .xij. *l.*

129. Rogerus, filius Ricardi Vet[u]le, est heres .j. carrucate terre in Herpingham, que est de feodo Willelmi de Edisfeld', que valet .iiij. *l.* cum instauramento .j. carruce: et ipse est in custodia matris sue et patruorum suorum per Dominum Regem, et est .vj. annorum; et mater sua habet .ij. filios et .v. filias. Et predictus Rogerus est nepos Gwidonis Buteturte, et cognatus Willelmi de Edisfeld', et mater sua est .xxx. annorum.

130. Agnes de Mundauill' habet villulam que vocatur Hornedes in dote de baronia Humfredi de Buhun. Eadem villa valet annuatim .x. *l.* cum instauramento .ij. carrucarum: et ipsa et .iij. pueri sui sunt in custodia Domini Regis, et primogenitus filius ejus est .xiiij. annorum, et fuit filius Teodbaldi Hautin et nepos Alberti Greslei. Et predicta Angnes (*sic*) est .xl. annorum.

131. Simon, filius Willelmi Buteriz, est in custodia Domini Regis, cui Eustacius filius Stephani dedit filiam suam per licenciam Domini Regis; et habuit custodiam predicti Simonis et terre sue in Wiuertone per .vij. annos. Predicta terra valet .xviij. *l.* per annum cum hoc instauramento, scilicet, .ij. carrucis de .viij. bobus, et .vj. equis, quolibet de .iij. *s.*, et .c. et .xl. ovibus; et si apponerentur .lx. oves, terra valeret .xviij. *l.* et .x. *s.*

[xl] Corrected by Round, *RD*, 54, n. 3.

Happing Hundred

127. Agnes de Mountchesney has 16 librates of land in Sutton in Happing Hundred of the fee of Roger Bigod.

128. Richard of Colkirk held the vill of Hempstead, which is half a knight's fee, in the same hundred, and he used to hold it in chief of the Lord King, and he (Richard) died. Geoffrey Peche married his (Richard's) widow with Hugh de Cressy's permission. A certain niece of the said Richard remained the heir there, and Roger de St. Denis married her with Hugh de Cressy's permission, and thus he (Roger) holds that land, which is worth £12.[168]

(South Erpingham Hundred)

129. Roger, son of Richard la Veile, is the heir to one carrucate of land in Erpingham, which belongs to the fee of William of Edgefield, and it is worth £4 with stock of one plough-team; and, with the Lord King's permission, he is in the wardship of his mother and his kinsfolk, and he is 6 years of age. His mother has two sons and five daughters. The said Roger is a nephew of Guy Buteturte and related to William of Edgefield, and his mother is 30.[169]

130. Agnes of Amundeville has the little vill called Oxnead in dower of the barony of Humphrey de Bohun. The same vill is worth £10 per annum with stock of 2 plough-teams. She and her three sons are in the Lord King's wardship, and the eldest son is 14 years of age, and was the son of Theobald Hautein and nephew of Albert Grelley. The aforesaid Agnes is 40.[170]

(Holt Hundred)

131. Simon, son of William Buteri, is in ward to the Lord King. Eustace fitz Stephen gave his daughter in marriage to him with licence from the Lord King; and he (Eustace) had wardship of the said Simon and his land in Wiveton for seven years. The said land is worth £18 per annum with the following stock: viz. 2 plough-teams of 8 oxen (each), 6 horses, each worth 3s, and 140 sheep. And if 60 sheep were added the land would be worth £18 10s.[171]

---

[168] Here the marriages of the widow and her niece, as heir, seem to have been arranged through the custodian, Hugh de Cressy.

[169] See no. 112, where Roger is incorrectly called Richard.

[170] See no. 109.

[171] See no. 137.

132. Stowe, que est dos Matillis de Bidune, que fuit filia Thome filii Bernardi, valet annuatim .xj. *l.* et .xij. *s.* et .ij. *d.* cum hoc instauramento, scilicet, .ij. carrucis de .viij. bobus, et .vj. equis et .iiij. vaccis et .iiij.^xx. ovibus . . . . xv. et cum .ij. suibus et .j. verre; et si .cc. oves ibi apponerentur, que possent ibi esse, tunc [valeret] .xij. l. et .xv. *s.* et .viij. *d.* Hanc firmam recepit Thomas filius Bernardi .ij. annis, et recepit [inde] .iiij. *l.* et .iiij. *s.* de adquisitionibus. Et preterea Johannes de Bidune junior, .c. et .x. *s.* Eugenia uxor Thome filii Bernardi, qui^xli modo habet custodiam post mortem predicti Johannis cepit .xlv. *s.* et .vj. *d.* et firmam .j. anni, scilicet, .xj. *l.* et .xj. *s.* et .ij. *d.*

133. Lauretta Picot, que fuit uxor Hugonis de Burdeleis et filia Eustacii Picot, est de donatione Domini Regis, et est .xl. annorum, et habet .vj. filios et .ij. filias: et Willelmus, filius ejus et heres, est .xxvj. annorum. Ipsa habet medietatem villa de Sculeton' cum pertinenciis de Tumested', que valet annuatim .iiij. *l.* et .viij. *s.* et .x. *d.*, cum hoc instauramento, scilicet, .j. carruca de .vj. bobus et .ij. equis, et cum .vj. vaccis et .xl. ovibus; et additis .xx. ovibus et .iiij. vaccis et .iiij. suibus, terra valeret .c. *s.* et .xij. *d.* Hanc terram tenet Lauretta sicut hereditatem suam.

134. . . . . . . ^xliiRicardus Vet[ule] est per Dominum Regem in custodia patruorum suorum, et est .vj. annorum; et habet in hundredo de Holt .xxiiij. *s.* de redditu, quos pater suus habuit ex dono [Domini] Regis.

135. [Emme] de Langetot est de donatione Domini Regis, et est .lx. annorum, et habet in hundredo de Holt feodum .j. militis, et .iiij. partes feodi .j. militis, quas alii tenent. Dominium suum in Binetre valet .lx. *s.* annuatim cum instauramento .j. carruce de .iiij. bobus, et .ij. equis et .j. herzurio. Et in hundredo de Eimeford habet ipsa .ij. milites fefatos, et .ij. partes .j. militis.

136. . . . . C[okesfeldi]a . . . . habet in villa de Snuterleia, .xij. libratas terre, de feodo Willelmi de Warenn'.

---

^xli Corrected from "que" in MS.

^xlii The MS is very damaged from here to the end of the membrane.

(Wayland Hundred)

132. Stow (Bedon), which is the dower of Matilda de Bidun, who was a daughter of Thomas fitz Bernard, is worth £11 12s 2d per annum with the following stock: viz. 2 plough-teams of 8 oxen (each?), 6 horses, 4 cows, and 80 sheep . . . 15, and with 2 sows and one boar; and if 200 sheep were added, which there could be, then it would be worth £12 15s 8d. Thomas fitz Bernard took this farm for two years, and received £4 4s from acquisitions.[172] Besides this, John de Bidun Junior (used to receive) 110s.[173] Moreover, after John's death Eugenia, Thomas fitz Bernard's widow, who now has wardship, took 45s 6d and the farm of one year, viz. £11 11s 2d. (*sic*)

133. Lauretta Picot, widow of Hugh de Burdeleis and daughter of Eustace Picot, is in the Lord King's gift, is 40 years of age, and has six sons and two daughters. William, her son and heir, is 26 years of age. She herself has half the vill of Scoulton with the appurtenances of Thompson, which is worth £4 8s 10d per annum with the following stock: viz. one plough-team of 6 oxen and 2 horses, 6 cows, and 40 sheep. With the addition of 20 sheep, 4 cows, and 4 sows the land would be worth 101s. Lauretta holds this land as her inheritance.

(Holt Hundred)

134. (Roger, son of)[174] . . . Richard la Veile is, with the Lord King's permission, in the wardship of his kinsmen and is 6 years of age; and in Holt Hundred he has 24s from rent, which his father had by gift of the Lord King.[175]

135. (Emma)[176] . . . de Langetot is in the Lord King's gift, is 60 years of age and has one and three-quarters knights' fees in Holt Hundred, which others hold. Her demesne in Bintree is worth 60s per annum with stock of one plough-team of 4 oxen, 2 horses, and one harrow-beast. In Eynsford Hundred she has 2 enfeoffed knights and two-thirds of one knight.

136. . . .(Cocksfield) . . . has in the vill of Sniterle[177] 12 librates of land of the fief of William de Warenne.

---

[172] I.e. in addition to the farm.

[173] The absence of a verb makes the meaning unclear; probably "used to receive" should be understood. See no. 114.

[174] See no. 129.

[175] From this entry to the end of the Norfolk rotulet the MS is very damaged.

[176] See nos. 90 and 99.

[177] *Alias* Blakeney, Holt Hundred: Round, *RD*, 56, n. 4, where he also suggests that 'c' and 'a' are the first and last letters of the "Cokesfeldia" (Cockfield) family, which held of the Warennes.

137. . . . . . . Will' Buterich' habet in hundredo de Eineford' terram que valet .c. *s.* annuatim cum hoc instauramento, scilicet, .iiij. bobus, .ij. equis, .j. herzerio.

138. [Willelmus] Tresgoz, filius Gaufridi de Tresgoz, est nepos Roberti de Gres-ley, et in custodia Domini Regis, et per eum fuit in custodia Roberti de Lucy cum terra sua . . . . . . per octo annos; que terra fuit jurata ad valenciam .xv. *l.*, sed Robertus posuit eam ad firmam pro .xx. *l.* cum instauramento .j. carruce: et si apponerentur .iiij. vacce et .c. oves, terra valeret .xxj. *l.* et .iiij. *s.*: et dictus Simon (*sic*) est [.xvii.] annorum.[xliii]

139. . . . . . . Reinham, qui est in custodia Eustachii filii Stephani, valet annuatim .vj.[xx.] *s.*, quos predictus Eustachius recepit hiis .viij. annis.

Hundredum de Galeho

140. [Filius Thome de Bella Fago est] in custodia Domini Regis, et per eum in custodia Nigelli filii Alexandri, et est .ij. annorum et dimidii, cum Crek, terra sua; de qua . . . . . . recepit, postquam habuit custodiam, .xvj. *m.* et .vij. *s.* et .iij. *d.* de omnibus exitibus; et habuit custodiam per annum et quantum . . . . . . diebus ante festum Sancti Botulfi. Hoc est instauramentum, scilicet, .ij. boves, .j. vacca, .vij. equi et .xxxj. oves; et valet cum instauramento .x. *l.*: et additis .ij. bobus et .v. vaccis et .x. porcis et .cc. ovibus, valebit villa .xv. *l.*

[xliii] The correct name is "Willelmus," aged 17: see nos. 195 and 197.

(Eynsford Hundred)

137. (Simon, son of). . .William Buteri has land in Eynsford Hundred that is worth 100s per annum with the following stock: viz. 4 oxen, 2 horses, and one harrow-beast.[178]

138. (William) Tresgoz, son of Geoffrey de Tresgoz and nephew of Robert Grelley, is in ward to the Lord King, and through him in the wardship of Robert de Lucy, with his land . . . (of Billingford) . . . for eight years, which land was sworn to be worth £15, but Robert put it at farm for £20 with stock of one plough-team; and if 4 cows and 100 sheep were added the land would be worth £21 4s. And Simon (*recte* William) is (17) years old.[179]

(Brothercross Hundred)

139. (Simon, son of William Buteri) . . . Raynham, which is in the wardship of Eustace fitz Stephen, is worth 120s per annum, which the aforesaid Eustace received for these (past) eight years.[180]

Gallow Hundred

140. (The son of Thomas de Belfou is) in the Lord King's wardship and through him in the wardship of Nigel fitz Alexander and is two and a half years of age, together with his land of Creake, from which, after he had wardship, (Nigel?) received 16 marks and 7s 3d from all sources; and he had wardship for a year and *quantum* (?)[181] . . . days before the feast of Saint Botolph.[182] This is the stock, viz. 2 oxen, one cow, 7 horses, and 31 sheep, and with this stock it is worth £10. With the addition of 2 oxen, 5 cows, 10 pigs, and 200 sheep the vill will be worth £15.[183]

---

[178] For the identification of Simon see no. 131.

[179] Round, *RD*, 57, n. 2, is of importance in providing the heir's correct name and the name of the manor.

[180] Brief though it is, this entry represents one of the clearest cases for an 8-year period between two sets of enquiries. The 1177 pipe roll confirms that the king had placed Eustace fitz Stephen in control of William Buteri's land in the Giffard Honour: *Pipe Roll 23 Henry II*, 164.

[181] Possibly for *quartam*.

[182] 17 June.

[183] See no. 49, where Alice, Thomas de Belfou's widow, is aged 20 and her son 3, and no. 105, where she is 20 and her son 2 years of age.

141. [Alicia que fuit uxor Thome de Bello] Fago est .xx. annorum, et fuit filia W[aleranni] de [Oiri] et neptis Nigelli filii Alexandri, et in ejus custodia per [Dominum Regem].

142. . . . . . [est in cust]odia Domini Regis[xliv] et per eum in custodia Eliensis episcopi .vj. annorum.

143. Clare que fuit Agnetis de Munchenesy est in . . . . .[xlv] scilicet, de festo S. Michaelis et de dicta villa ceperunt servientes nunc .lij. *s.* et .vi. *d.* quos expenderunt in [vic]tu famulorum. Hoc est instauramentum dicte ville: .ij. carruce de .viij. bobus et .iiij. caballi et .j. vacca.

144. . . . . . . [vil]la valet .vij. *l.* Et additis .cc. ovibus ipsa valeret .ix. *l.*

De dominabus et puellis que sunt de maritagio Regis

[Rot. 7.]

Primus rotulus de Sudfolk', de dominabus et pueris et puellis

145. Gilebertus, filius Walteri Pikardi, qui est .xx. annorum, est in custodia Domini Regis cum terra sua, quam Gilebertus de Ver habuit in custodia sua jam .viij. annis elapsis, et omnes exitus inde recepit. Terra sua valet .xx. *s.* cum hoc instauramento, scilicet, .xx. ovibus et .ij. vaccis et .ij. equis; et hoc servicium debet terra Domino Regi, scilicet, .j. arcum et sagittas, et .j. gladium et .j. saccum cum brocca, ad servitium Domini Regis, cum ierit cum exercitu in Walliam.

146. Mabilia de Heliun, que est .lx. annorum, est de donatione Domini Regis, cujus heres est Robertus de Heliun; et ipsa fuit filia Rogeri filii Ricardi. Terra sua quam tenet in dote valet annuatim .c. *s.* cum hoc instauramento, scilicet, .xl. ovibus, .vj. bobus, .ij. equis, .ij. suibus, et .j. verre.

[xliv] From here to the end of the rotulet is omitted from Harl. MS 624 and Grimaldi, *Rotuli de Dominabus*. Round no doubt applied an ink restorer, which apparently he used on the roll for Suffolk (*RD*, 65, n. 1), to produce the remainder of entry 142 and the following two entries, but they are illegible now, even with the aid of an ultra-violet lamp.

[xlv] Although not indicated by Round, a word or two seems to be missing here, possibly "custodia" or "manu".

141. (Alice, widow of Thomas de Belfou) is 20 and was a daughter of Waleran de (Oiri) and a niece of Nigel fitz Alexander, and in his wardship through (the Lord King).

142 . . . is in the wardship of the Lord King and through him in the wardship of the bishop of Ely for 6 years.

(South Greenhoe Hundred)

143. [Cockley] Cley which belonged to Agnes de Mountchesney is in (wardship?), viz. from Michaelmas, and the serjeants took 52s 6d from the said vill, which they spent on victuals for the household servants. This is the stock of the vill: 2 plough-teams of 8 oxen (each), 4 horses, and one cow.

144. . . . the vill is worth £7. With an additional 200 sheep it would be worth £9.

Concerning ladies and girls who are in the Lord King's marriage gift

[Roll 7.]

First roll for Suffolk concerning ladies, boys and girls[184]

(Risbridge Hundred)

145. Gilbert fitz Walter Picard, who is 20, is in ward to the Lord King, together with his land, which Gilbert de Vere held in wardship for the past eight years receiving all the proceeds from it. His land is worth 20s with the following stock: viz. 20 oxen, 2 cows, and 2 horses. The land owes the following service to the Lord King, viz. one bow with arrows, one sword, and one sack with a clasp for the Lord King's use, when he goes with his army into Wales.[185]

146. Mabel de Helion, 60, whose heir is Robert de Helion, is in the Lord King's gift, and she was the daughter of Roger fitz Richard. Her land, which is held in dower, is worth 100s per annum with the following stock: viz. 40 sheep, 6 oxen, 2 horses, 2 sows, and one boar.[186]

---

[184] This implies that there was at least another roll for Suffolk, as there was for Buckinghamshire, Essex, and probably Cambridgeshire.

[185] This minor serjeanty tenure does not appear in Round, *The King's Serjeants*. The property was at Great Wratting, Risbridge Hundred: Round, *RD*, 59, n. 1.

[186] The property was probably Haverhill, Risbridge Hundred: Round, *RD*, 59, n. 2.

Hundredum de Laford'

147. In Ykinlingham tenet Walterus filius Willelmi unam terram de feodo Stephani de Bellocampo; unde reddit .xlij. *d*. Osberto de Glanuill', qui habet custodiam terre predicti Stephani cum herede.

Marginal note: d.

Hundredum de Babeng'

148. Heres Radulfi de Haudebouill', qui nondum est unius anni, est in custodia Domini Regis, et per eum in custodia Rannulfi de Glanuill', cum .ij. partibus ville de Aketone, que valent annuatim .xx. *l*.; et terciam partem predicte ville habet uxor que fuit predicti Radulfi, que est neptis Rannulfi de Glanuill', et in ejus custodia.

149. Amfrida de Winemersse, que est .lx. annorum, est in donatione Domini Regis. Terra ejus valet .xx. *s*.; et habet .vij. infantes et heres ejus est .xviij. annorum.

150. Leticia, que fuit uxor Willelmi filii Mabilie, que est .lx. annorum, est in donatione Domini Regis, et terra ejus valet .iiij. *l*. annuatim, et est soror Willelmi de Kiueli.

151. Cristiana, que fuit uxor Warengerii de Hocxene, est .l. annorum, et est in donatione Domini Regis; et ipsa tenet dimidiam carrucatam terre in Denham pro .iij. *d*., qui dantur ad firmam Regis, et valet .j. *m*. per annum; et preterea, ipsa tenet .vj. acras pro .ij. *s*. de episcopo Norwicensi; et de Walkelino Archidiacono tenet ipsa .v. solidatas terre, et valet dim. *m*. annuatim. Et habet filium heredem, qui est .xviij. annorum, et preter eum .iij. filias.

Marginal note: d.[xlvi]

152. Matillis, que fuit uxor Philippi de Columbariis, est in donatione Domini Regis, et est .xl. annorum; et filius suus est .xviij. annorum, et est cum Rege; et ipsa habet .xl. solidatas redditus in villa de Akholt, et puer habet terram per Dominum Regem.

[xlvi] Omitted from Round, *RD*, 60.

Lackford Hundred

147. In Icklingham Walter fitz William holds one piece of land of the fee of Stephen de Beauchamp, from which he renders 42d to Osbert Glanvill, who has wardship of the said Stephen's land, together with the heir.[187]

(*Marginal note*: d.)

Babergh Hundred

148. The heir of Ralph de Hodeboville, who is not yet one year old, is in ward to the Lord King and through him in the wardship of Rannulf Glanvill, with two-thirds of the vill of Acton, which is worth £20 per annum. Ralph's widow, a niece of Rannulf Glanvill, has one-third of the vill and she is in his wardship.

149. Amfrid of Withermarsh, who is 60, is in the Lord King's gift. Her land is worth 20s, and she has seven children, and the heir is 18.

150. Leticia, widow of William fitz Mabel, is 60 and is in the Lord King's gift. Her land is worth £4 per annum, and she is a sister of William de Kiveli.[188]

(Hoxne Hundred)[189]

151. Christiana, widow of Warenger of Hoxne, is 50 and is in the Lord King's gift. She holds half a carrucate of land in Denham for 3d, which is paid to the Lord King's farm, and it is worth one mark per annum. She also has 6 acres for 2s from the bishop of Norwich, and 5 solidates of land from Walklin, the archdeacon, and it is worth half a mark per annum. She has a son and heir, who is 18, and in addition to him she has three daughters.

(*Marginal note*: d.)

(Hartismere Hundred)

152. Matilda, widow of Philip de Columbières, is in the Lord King's gift and is 40. Her son is 18 and is with the Lord King. She has 40 solidates of rents in the vill of Occold, and her son holds his land through the Lord King.

---

[187] Osbert Glanvill was Rannulf Glanvill's brother, who assumed a number of wardships on the death of Gilbert de Coleville: see entries 153, 173, and 200.

[188] William de Kiveli held land in serjeanty at Boreham, Chelmsford Hundred, Essex: Round, *RD*, 60, n. 3.

[189] Bishop's Hundred in Domesday Book.

Hundredum de Karleford'

153. Heres Stephani de Bellocampo fuit in custodia Domini Regis anno preterito a Dominica Passionis Domini illius anni usque ad festum Apostolorum Simonis et Jude, cum villa de Clopton'; et per Dominum Regem fuit in custodia Gileberti de Coleuill' toto predicto termino, qui interim inde cepit de uno homine pertinente ad predictam terram .ij. *m.* Hec terra cum dicto herede est modo in custodia Osberti de Glanuill', et valet annuatim .vj. *l.* cum hoc instauramento, scilicet, .j. carruca de .viij. bobus, et .ij. equis et .j. herzerio et .ij. vaccis et .iii. suibus et .j. verre et .xx. ovibus, et plus instauramenti non potest sustinere, nec firma augeri. Heres predicti Stephani fuit .iiij. annorum ad Pascha proximo preteritum.

154. Matillis, que fuit uxor Gileberti de Coleuill', et filia Roberti de Boseuill', est de donatione Domini Regis, et in custodia Rannulfi de Glanuill'. Et habet de maritagio in hundredo de Hertesmere, de feodo Stephani de Muntchenesi, .vij. libratas reddituum, et est .xxvij. annorum, et heres suus est .xij. annorum et in custodia Rannulfi de Glanuill'.

155. Eadem Matillis habet in hundredo de Colenexe in villa de Faltham unam terram, que valet annuatim .iiij. *l.,* et est de feodo Rogeri Bigot; et ipsa habet .ij. filios et .vj. filias.

156. Alexandria, mater Gileberti de Coleuill', est in donatione Domini Regis, et est .lx. annorum. Terra sua in Kenint' valet per annum .xx. *s.*

157. Eadem Alexandria tenet .xx. solidatas in Keneton ad firmam, que fuerunt Gileberti de Coleuill' filii sui, et respondet inde custodi predicti Gileberti; et hoc est instauramentum, scilicet, .vj. boves, .ij. equi, .j. hercerius, nec potest plus pati. Terra predicti Gileberti in Gategraue reddit per annum .xj. *s.* Terra sua in Campesse reddit per annum .iiij. *s.* et vj. *d.*

Carlford Hundred

153. The heir of Stephen de Beauchamp was in the Lord King's wardship in the last year, from Passion Sunday of that year until the feast of the apostles Simon and Jude,[190] together with the vill of Clopton; and through the Lord King he was in the wardship of Gilbert de Coleville the whole of that term, and the latter took 2 marks in this period from one man belonging to this land. This land, together with the heir, is now in the wardship of Osbert Glanvill and it is worth £6 per annum with the following stock: viz. one plough-team of 8 oxen, 2 horses, one beast for harrowing, 2 cows, 3 sows, one boar, and 20 sheep, and no more stock can be sustained, nor can the farm be increased. Stephen's heir was 4 years old last Easter.[191]

(Hartismere Hundred)

154. Matilda, widow of Gilbert de Coleville and daughter of Robert of Boseville, is in the Lord King's gift and in the wardship of Rannulf Glanvill. From her marriage portion in Hartismere Hundred, of the fee of Stephen de Mountchesney, she has 7 librates in rents.[192] She is 27 and her heir is 12 and in the wardship of Rannulf Glanvill.

(Colneis Hundred)

155. The same Matilda has one property in the vill of Falkenham in Colneis Hundred which is worth £4 per annum and is of the fee of Roger Bigod. She has two sons and six daughters.

(Loes Hundred)

156. Alexandria, mother of Gilbert de Coleville, is in the Lord King's gift, and is 60. Her land in Kenton is worth 20s per annum.

157. The same Alexandria has 20 solidates in Kenton at farm, which belonged to her son, Gilbert de Coleville, and she is answerable for it to Gilbert's custodian (Rannulf Glanville). This is the stock: viz. 6 oxen, 2 horses, and one beast for harrowing; and it is not possible to sustain more. The land of the said Gilbert in Gedgrave renders 11s per annum. His land in Campsey renders 4s 6d per annum.

---

[190] From 18 March to 28 October 1184.

[191] See no. 173.

[192] The land may have been in Wyverstone or Westhorpe, Hartismere Hundred.

158. Filius Alberti de Gresley est in custodia Domini Regis, et habet .iij. sorores, que sunt infra etatem, et ipse .xj. annorum.

159. Herebertus, filius Rollandi, tenuit terram suam de Rege, sicut joculator, et habuit in hundredo de Bosemere .xxx. acras, quas uxor ejus, que est .xl. annorum, et heres suus, qui est .xiij. annorum, tenent. Uxor fuit filia Walteri de Heccham, et habet .v. filias preter filium.

160. Margareta Comitissa est de donatione Domini Regis, et est .xl. annorum, et comes Britannie habet filiam suam, et ipsa habet .j. filium de Humfrido de Buun', qui est infra etatem. Ipsa tenet villam de Wissint' in dote et valet annuatim .xx- viij. *l.* Predicta villa fuit seisita in manum Domini Regis a festo Ascensionis Domini usque ad Ad Vincula Sancti Petri, et interim recepit inde Rannulfus de Glanuill' .l. *s.*

161. Matillis de Beauerio est de donatione Domini Regis, et est .l. annorum, et Willelmus de Beauerio est filius ejus. Ipsa tenet Crateleford' in maritagio, et valet annuatim .x. *l.*

162. Hubertus Blundus, filius Willelmi Blundi, est in custodia Domini Regis, et per eum fuit ipse et terra sua jam per .viij. annos in custodia Eliensis episcopi, et ipse est .xx. annorum, et fuit nepos Huberti de Muntchenesy. Terra sua de Yxewurth' venit in manum episcopi ad festum Sancti Michaelis post mortem Sarre de Muntchenesy. Et valet predicta villa .xv. *l.* cum instauramento quod ibi est, scilicet, .xij. bobus et .iiij. equis et .j. hercerio; et si apponerentur .cc. oves et .vj.

158. The son of Albert Grelley is in the Lord King's wardship and he has three sisters who are minors, and he is 11 years old.[193]

(Bosmere Hundred)

159. Herbert fitz Roland held his land of the the Lord King as a jester, and in Bosmere Hundred held 30 acres which his widow, who is 40, and his heir, who is 13, hold. The widow was a daughter of Walter of Heccham, and she has five daughters besides the son.[194]

(Blything Hundred)

160. Countess Margaret is in the Lord King's gift and is 40. The count of Brittany is married to her daughter, and she has by Humphrey de Bohun a son who is a minor. She holds the vill of Wisset in dower, and it is worth £28 per annum. The said vill was seized into the Lord King's hand from the feast of the Ascension to Saint Peter ad Vincula,[195] and in this period Rannulf Glanvill received 50s from it.

161. Matilda *de Beaverio* is in the Lord King's gift and is 50.[196] William *de Beaverio* is her son. She holds Cratfield as her marriage portion, and it is worth £10 per annum.

(Blackbourn Hundred)

162. Hubert Blund, son of William Blund, is in ward to the Lord King and through the Lord King he and his land have been in the wardship of the bishop of Ely for eight years. He is 20 and a nephew of Hubert de Mountchesney. His land in Ixworth came into the bishop's hand at the Michaelmas after the death of Sarah de Mountchesney. The said vill is worth £15 (per annum) with the existing stock, namely 12 oxen, 4 horses, and one harrow-beast; and if 200 sheep, 6 cows, one

---

[193] For further references to the son, widow, and nephew of Albert Grelley see nos. 7, 15, 28, 111, and 130. This is an unusual entry in that there is no reference to property, livestock, or values. The Grelleys held land at Willisham and Blakenham in Bosmere Hundred: Round, *RD*, 62, n. 2.

[194] Hemingstone, Bosmere Hundred: Round, *RD*, 62, n. 3.

[195] From 10 May to 1 August 1184. See also no. 216, where there are further references to the two children. Entries 8 and 12 do not refer to her children.

[196] The same Matilda as in no. 2, where she is said to be 60: Round, *RD*, 63, n. 1.

vacce et .j. taurus et .iiij. sues et .j. verris, tunc valeret manerium .xvij. *l*. et .x. *s*. Bailiui episcopi receperunt de dicta villa de firma, ad festum Omnium Sanctorum, .xiiij. *s*. et .iii. *d*. et *ob*.; ad Natale, .xl. *s*. et .iiij. *d*. et *ob*. ; ad Pascha, .xlj. *s*. et .iii. *d*.; ad Pentecosten, .iiij. *s*. et .iii. *d*. et *ob*.; et de gersumiis, .lx. *s*., et de aliis fortunis, .xj. *s*. et .vj. *d*.; et heres per preceptum episcopi recepit .xl. *s*. de auxiliis.

[Rot. 7. d.]

163. Esfeldia et Walesham' sunt maneria predicti Huberti Blundi et fuerunt Willelmi patris sui, et fuerunt in manu Eliensis episcopi cum herede .viii. annis; et reddunt modo annuatim .xxxj. *l*. cum instauramento .ij. carrucarum, que sunt apud Walesham, de .xvj. bobus, et .v. equis et cum .vj. vaccis et .j. tauro et .c. ovibus et .v. suibus et .j. verre; et cum .ij. carrucis, que sunt apud Esfeld', de .xij. bobus, et .v. equis et .vj. vaccis et .j. tauro et .c. ovibus et .v. suibus et .j. verre; et predicte ville non possunt plus instauramenti sustinere, nec plus valere. In primo anno de hiis .viii. annis elapsis recepit episcopus Eliensis de illis .ij. maneriis .x. *l*. et .v. *s*. Et in secundo anno sequenti recepit idem episcopus de hiisdem maneriis .xj. *l*. et .xix. *s*. et .ix. *d*., tam de firma quam de perquisitis. Tertio autem anno recepit ipse inde .xxiij. *l*. et .xix. *s*. et .ix. *d*., tam de firma quam de perquisitis. In quarto vero anno, idem inde [recepit] .xx. *l*. et .vj. *s*. et .viij. *d*., tam de firma quam de per-quisitis, et de bladis venditis et omnibus modis. Preterea episcopus habuit eodem anno de Westleston', que illo anno cecidit in manum episcopi ad opus heredis (*sic*).[xlvii] In quinto vero anno recepit episcopus de dictis .ij. maneriis xx. *l*. et .iiij. *s*. et iiij. *d*., de omnibus exitibus; et preterea de Westleston' .vj . *l*. In .vj^{to}. quidem anno recepit episcopus de dictis .ii. maneriis .xxj. *l*. et .ij. *s*. et .v. *d*., de omnibus exitibus; et preterea de Westleston' .vj. *l*. In septimo autem anno posuit episcopus predicta .ij. maneria ad firmam pro .xxxvij. *l*., cum vj. *l*. de Westleston, quam firmam idem episcopus recepit. In octavo quidem anno, scilicet, in presenti, recepit episcopus medietatem firme sue de .ij. terminis jam preteritis, scilicet, .xv. *l*. et .x. *s*.; et preterea .iij. *l*. de Westleston'. Preterea homines utriusque manerii dederunt heredi Willelmi Blundi, ad auxilia, .viij. *m*.

[xlvii] It seems that an amount, presumably £6, has been omitted. Harl. MS 624 makes the rare marginal comment: "Non dicitur quantum tunc habuerit."

bull, 4 sows, and one boar were added then the manor would be worth £17 10s. From the farm of the said manor the bishop's bailiffs received 14s 3½d at the feast of All Saints, 40s 4½d at Christmas, 41s 3d at Easter, 4s 3½d at Pentecost, and 60s from marriage fines, and 11s 6d from other sources. And the heir received 40s in aids by order of the bishop.[197]

[Roll 7. dorse.]

(Blackbourn Hundred)

163. Ashfield and Walsham are manors of the abovementioned Hubert Blund and belonged to William, his father. They were in the bishop of Ely's hand together with the heir for eight years. At present they render £31 per annum with stock of 2 plough-teams, which are at Walsham, with 16 oxen, 5 horses, 6 cows, one bull, 100 sheep, 5 sows, and one boar; and 2 plough-teams, which are at Ashfield, with 12 oxen, 5 horses, 6 cows, one bull, 100 sheep, 5 sows, and one boar. And the said manors cannot sustain any more stock or be worth more. In the first of these eight years the bishop of Ely received from those two manors £10 5s; in the second year the same bishop received £11 19s 9d, from both the farm and the perquisites (of court); then in the third year he received £23 19s 9d from both the farm and perquisites; and in the fourth year he received £20 6s 8d from the farm, perquisites, the sale of grain, and from all other sources. Furthermore, the bishop had (£6) in the same year from Westleton, which came into his possession for the support of the heir. In the fifth year the bishop received from the two manors £20 3s 4d from all sources, and a further £6 from Westleton; in the sixth year the bishop received from the two manors £21 2s 5d from all sources, as well as £6 from Westleton. In the seventh year the bishop placed the two manors at farm for £37, including £6 from Westleton, which farm the same bishop received. In the eighth and current year the bishop received half of his farm from the past two terms, viz. £15 10s and £3 from Westleton. Furthermore the men of both manors have given William Blund's heir 8 marks in aids.[198]

---

[197] In this entry (and no. 122) no distinction is made between *villa* and *manerium*. For the genealogy of the Mountchesney family see Round, *RD*, xlv.

[198] This is one of the clearest accounts of the fortunes of an heir's estates year by year in the eight-year period which separates the two supposed enquiries. These two manors seem to have prospered quite considerably.

164. Hubertus de Muntchenesy fuit in custodia Domini Regis et per eum in custodia Eliensis episcopi, cum terra sua de Stretford', que est de baronia Henrici de Essex', quam Dominus Rex ei restituit ad proximum Pascha. Et episcopus Eliensis recepit inde annuatim, dum habuit custodiam, .viij. *l.*

Hundredum de Lose

165. Stauerton' et Clakestorp et Parva Farlingham sunt de honore de Eya. Stauerton', ex qua fuit in manu Domini Regis et vicecomitis, reddidit annuatim de firma .xx. *l.*, cum hoc instauramento, scilicet, .vj. bobus, .j. equo, .iiij. vaccis et .iiij. suibus et .lx. ovibus; et si adderentur .lx. oves, villa valeret annuatim .xx. *l.* et .x. *s.*; et precipitur instaurari. Preter firmam recepit vicecomes intra hos .viij. annos .ij. *m.*, et annuatim .xx. gallinas, et de Adam de Eik .iij. *m.* pro forefacto.

166. Clakestorp reddidit annuatim .vij. *l.* et .ij. *s.* de firma. Et preterea recepit Jodlenus de placitis .v. *s.*, et .iij. *s.* de gersumis. Preterea .xiiij. acre de guastiva sunt in dominio, que nullum unquam fecerunt servicium.

167. Parva Farlingham reddidit annuatim .ix. *l.* cum hoc instauramento, scilicet, .vj. bobus et .j. equo; et non potest plus pati instauramenti, nec plus valere. Preterea homines dederunt vicecomiti annuatim infra hos .viij. annos .j. *m.* preter firmam.

Endorsed:[xlviii] Rotulus de dominabus, pueris et puellis de .xij. comitatibus, scilicet, de Middelsex et Essex, Hertfordsira et Bedefordsira et Bukinghamsira, et Norfolk et Sudfolk, Cantebrigesira, Huntedunesira, Norhantunsira, Roteland et Lincolnsira de itinere Hugonis de Morewich, Radulfi Murdac et Willelmi Vavassoris et Magistri Thome de Hesseburn'.

[xlviii] The endorsement is virtually illegible, but presumably it was not when first transcribed.

(Samford Hundred)

164. Hubert de Mountchesney[199] was in ward to the Lord King and through him was in the wardship of the bishop of Ely, together with his land of Stratford, which belongs to the barony of Henry of Essex,[200] which the Lord King restored to him (Hubert) last Easter. While he had wardship the bishop of Ely received £8 per annum from there.

(Loes Hundred)

165. Staverton, *Clakestorp*,[201] and Little Framlingham belong to the honour of Eye. From the time that it was in the Lord King's and sheriff's hands Staverton rendered a farm of £20 per annum, with the following stock: viz. 6 oxen, one horse, 4 cows, 4 sows, and 60 sheep; and if 60 sheep were added the vill would be worth £20 10s; and it was ordered to be stocked. Besides the farm the sheriff received in these eight years 2 marks and 20 hens per annum, and from Adam of Eik a fine of 3 marks.

166. *Clakestorp* rendered £7 2s per annum from the farm. Furthermore, Jodlen received 5s from pleas, and 3s from marriage fines. In addition, there are 14 acres of waste in demesne, which have never rendered any service.

167. Little Framlingham rendered £9 per annum with the following stock: viz. 6 oxen and one horse; and it is not possible to sustain more stock, nor can it be worth more. Furthermore, besides the farm the men have given 8 marks per annum to the sheriff for these (past) eight years.[202]

Endorsement: roll concerning widows, boys, and girls of twelve shires, viz. of Middlesex, Essex, Hertfordshire, Bedfordshire, Buckinghamshire, Norfolk, Suffolk, Cambridgeshire, Huntingdonshire, Northamptonshire, Rutland, and Lincolnshire from the eyre of Hugh de Morwich, Ralph Murdac, William Vavassor, and Master Thomas of Hurstbourne.[203]

---

[199] Possibly the third son of Agnes de Montchesney, who was a clerk, according to no. 116.

[200] The barony of Henry of Essex had escheated to the Crown in 1163.

[201] The unidentified *Clachestorp* in Domesday Book.

[202] Entries 165–167 are struck out in the MS and are followed by four entries, which in turn have been erased.

[203] The endorsement, which is now illegible, provides good evidence of the coherence of the rolls and the constitution of the eyre. Much depends of course on the dating of the endorsement, but Round did not deal with this issue. This group of four justices appears together again under *Nova placita et nova conventiones* in *Pipe Roll 32 Henry II*, 27, 35, 65, 77; W. L. Warren, *Henry II*, 295, n. 6.

[Rot. 8.]

Rotulus de dominabus, pueris et puellis de Hertford'sire

Verum dictum de Hundredo de Bradewatre

168. Comitissa de Hybernia est de donatione Domini Regis. Weston', que est de dote sua, valet annuatim .xv. *l.* cum instauramento quod ibi est, scilicet, .iij. carrucis et .ix. vaccis et .ij. suibus et .j. verre et .xxviij. ovibus; et si essent ibi .v. carruce et .ij. equi herzorii et .x. vacce et .j. taurus et .x. sues et .j. verris et .cc. oves, que omnia possent ibi esse, dicta villa valeret per annum .xx. *l.*

Marginal note: d.

169. Clemencia, que fuit uxor Huberti de Sancto Claro, est de donatione Domini Regis, et est .iiii^{ter}.xx. annorum. Terra sua in Weston' valet .iiij. *l.*, .xij. *d.* minus; et si esset instaurata de dimidia^{xlix} carrucata et .xl. ovibus, dicta terra valeret per annum .c. *s.*

Hundredum de Hodeschae

170. Robertus de Habingwurthe tenuit .j. acram terre in Surreia, in Micheham, et quando dictus Robertus obiit occasione illius acre fuit totum tenementum ejus seisitum in manu Domini Regis cum herede suo, qui est leprosus, et est .xij. annorum, et in manu Roberti de Siflewast'. Robertus de Abbingburne habuit .ij. hidas et .j. virgatam terre in Walingt', que sunt in manu Domini Regis cum dicto herede. De .ij. predictarum hidarum^l et .j. virgata predicta et de .j. alia virgata terre in Chahale, que est de eodem feodo, recepit Henricus de Cornhil' ad opus Domini Regis per annum .xxx. *s.*, sine instauramento, de monachis Sancti Albani et de Willelmo de Wanlington'; et dicta hida et dimidia ita care fuerunt affirmate, ac si essent instaurate de .lx. ovibus et dimidia carruca.^{li} Aliam predictarum hidarum tenet Warinus de Bassingburn', per servicium militis quantum spectat ad .j. hidam. Et sunt dicte hide de feodo Rualdi pincerne.

---

^{xlix} MS: "dimia."

^l There has been a clumsy attempt at erasure and correction, but clearly the reference is to the 2 hides and 1 virgate. Grimaldi and Round read "De .i. predictarum hidarum."

^{li} Round, *RD*, 67: ". . . ac si essent instaurate de .lx. ovibus. Et dimidiam carrucatam aliam predictarum hidarum tenet Warinus . . ."

[Roll 8.]

Roll concerning ladies, boys, and girls of Hertfordshire

The Testimony of Broadwater Hundred

168. The countess of Ireland is in the Lord King's gift.[204] Weston, which is of her dower, is worth £15 per annum with the existing stock, viz. 3 plough-teams, 9 cows, 2 sows, one boar, and 28 sheep; and if there were 5 plough-teams and 2 horses for harrowing, 10 cows, one bull, 10 sows, one boar, and 200 sheep, which could all be there, the said vill would be worth £20 per annum.

(*Marginal note*: d.)

169. Clemence, widow of Hubert of Saint Clair, is in the Lord King's gift and is 80. Her land in Weston is worth £3 19s, and if it were stocked with half a plough-team and 40 sheep it would be worth 100s per annum.[205]

Odsey Hundred

170. Robert de Abbingworth held one acre of land in Mitcham, Surrey, and when the said Robert died, on account of that acre his whole tenement was seized into the Lord King's hand, together with the heir, who is a leper, twelve years of age, and he is held by Robert de Siflewast. Robert of Abbingburne held two hides and one virgate of land in Wallington, which are in the Lord King's hand with the said heir. From the above two hides and one virgate and from another virgate of land in Clayhall,[206] which is of the same fee, Henry of Cornhill[207] received 30s per annum, without stock, from the monks of Saint Albans and from William of Wallington for the Lord King's use. The said hide and a half (*sic*) were dearly farmed out, as if they were stocked with 60 sheep and half a plough-team. Warin of Bassingburne has another of the said hides for the knight-service appropriate to one hide. And the said hides belong to the fee of Ruald, the butler.[208]

---

[204] Eva of Leinster, widow of Richard "Strongbow," second earl of Pembroke.

[205] See no. 107, where Clemence appears as 60 years of age.

[206] Possibly Clothall, Odsey Hundred, in Domesday Book.

[207] Sheriff of London, 1187–1189, with Richard, son of Reiner.

[208] Round, *RD*, 67, n. 1, points out that this entry highlights the abuse of prerogative wardship, in that the tenure of one acre of land in Surrey in chief of the Crown subjected property in Hertfordshire to royal wardship. The entry is also discussed in Lally, "Secular Patronage," 165. The issue of prerogative wardship is also discussed in R. Bartlett, *England under the Norman and Angevin Kings, 1075–1225* (Oxford, 2000), 163. Cf. Magna Carta, cl. 37.

Hundredum de Herdford'

171. Agnes de Valeines est de donatione Domini Regis, et est .l. annorum. Terre sue, scilicet, Hortfordbur' et Hochwell', valent .xv. *l.* per annum cum instauramento quod ibi est, scilicet, .j. carruca apud Hortfordbur', et alia apud Holchwell', .v. vaccis et .lx. ovibus et .v. suibus; et si ibi essent .iiij. carruce et .c. oves et .x. vacce et .j. taurus et .x. sues et .j. verris, dicte terre valerent per annum .xx. *l.*

172. Matillis de Luuetot, que fuit filia Walteri filii Roberti et uxor Willelmi de Luuetot, est de donatione Domini Regis, et est .xxiiij. annorum; et habet de predicto Willelmo .j. filiam, que est .vij. annorum et in custodia Radulfi Murdac. Ipsa habet villam de Dinel' in dotem, que valet annuatim .xij. *l.* cum instauramento quod ibi est, scilicet, .ij. carrucis et .xxxvij. ovibus; et si esset ibi tertia carruca et .c. oves, villa valeret .xv. *l.*

[Rot. 8. d.]
Endorsed: De dominabus et eschaetis de Hertford'sire proinde

[Rot. 9.]

Rotulus de dominabus, pueris et puellis de Essex

173. Filius Stephani de Bello Campo est in custodia Domini Regis, et per ipsum in custodia Osberti de Glanuill', a festo Sancti Andree proximo preterito, et fuit .iiij. annorum ad Pascha proximo preteritum. Stephanus de Bello Campo obiit anno quo Ricardus Cantuariensis archiepiscopus obiit, ad festum Sancti Eadmundi. Terra sua de Lammersse cum pertinenciis seisita fuit in manum Domini Regis cum herede, et ad proximum Pascha sequens, liberata fuit custodia terre cum herede, sine instauramento, Gileberto de Coleuill', qui eam tenuit a Pascha

Hertford Hundred

171. Agnes de Valoynes is in the Lord King's gift and is 50 years of age.[209] Her lands, namely Hertingfordbury and Hockwellbury, are worth £15 per annum with the existing stock, viz. one plough-team at Hertingfordbury and another at Hockwellbury, 5 cows, 60 sheep, and 5 sows. And if there were three plough-teams, 100 sheep, 10 cows, one bull, 10 sows, and one boar the said property would be worth £20 per annum.

(Hitchin Hundred)

172. Matilda de Luvetot, daughter of Walter fitz Robert and widow of William de Luvetot, is in the Lord King's gift, and she is 24. By William she has one seven-year-old daughter, who is in the wardship of Ralph Murdac. She has the vill of Dinsley in dower, which is worth £12 per annum with the existing stock, viz. 2 plough-teams and 37 sheep; and if there were a third plough-team and 100 sheep the vill would be worth £15.

[Roll 8. dorse.]
Endorsement: Concerning ladies and escheats of Hertfordshire.

[Roll 9.]

Roll concerning ladies, boys, and girls of Essex

(Hinckford Hundred)

173. The son of Stephen de Beauchamp is in ward to the Lord King and through him in the wardship of Osbert Glanvill, since the feast of St. Andrew last past (30 November), and he was 3 years old last Easter. Stephen de Beauchamp died in the year that Richard, archbishop of Canterbury, died at the feast of St. Edmund.[210] His land at Lamarsh with its appurtenances was seized into the Lord King's hand with the heir, and at the following Easter (1184) wardship of the land and the heir was handed over, without stock, to Gilbert de Coleville who

---

[209] Her age is given as "more than 60" in nos. 193 and 226.

[210] This seems to confirm that the year prior to the enquiry was 1184. This St. Edmund's feast day was 20 November 1183: Round, *RD*, xxii.

usque ad .xv. dies post festum Sancti Michaelis proximum; qui interim cepit de
firma ville .x. *l.*, de Roberto de Bello Campo .v. *m.* et .xx. arietes, de Ricardo de
Bello Campo .v. *m.*, de Gaufrido de Bedeford' .xx. *s.*, de Ernaldo .iij. *m.* et .ij.
s. et .viij. *d.*, de Gaufrido preposito .ij. *m.* et .ij. porcos, de Rimilda vidua .xx. *s.*,
de Willelmo filio Wimarc' .xxj. *s.*, de Willelmo presbitero .j. *m.*, de Roberto
filio Goding' dim. *m.*, de Gileberto filio Hoin dim. *m.*, de Nicolao dim. *m.*,
de Radulfo Cristemesse .iij. *s.*, de Willelmo de Stura .iij. *s.*, de Nicolao Correui
.iij. *s.*, de Ailrico .viij. *s.* Et Simon de Haspahal' et Robertus Barat, servientes,
habuerunt .iiij. *s.* Dictus Stephanus habuit .iij. filias, quarum primogenita est .xiiij.
annorum. Post mortem Gileberti de Coleuill', tradidit Dominus Rex dictam
terram, cum herede, Osberto de Glanuill', ad festum, scilicet, Sancti Andree.
Quando Gilebertus de Coleuill' tenuit predictam villam, ipsa valebat annuatim
.xj. *l.* de firma, cum purcatiis, sine instauramento; et si esset instaurata de .v. carrucis et .ij. herzuriis, .xij. vaccis et .j. tauro, .x. suibus et .j. verre et .c. ovibus, villa
valeret annuatim .xxij. *l.*: et non potest plus instauramenti pati, nec plus valere,
quia terra est nimium fallians. Preter dictam villam habuit dictus Stephanus .j.
carrucatam terre in Hald'eh' quam habuit de purcatio, et reddebat inde redditum, unde superplusagium valet .j. *m.* argenti. In Fahirstiam, que est de eodem
feodo, sunt .vij. *s.* de asiso redditu, et .iij. *ob.*; et .j. carruca de .vj. bobus, et .ii.
equis et .j. herciorius (*sic*) et .ij. vacce et .ij. sues et .xx. oves, nec plus potest ibi esse
instauramenti; et cum hoc instauramento valet .lx. *s.* In Senesfeld' sunt .viij. *s.* de
asiso redditu, in Straford' sunt .vi. *s.* de asiso redditu. De eodem feodo Osbertus
de Glanuill' cepit de Ernaldo .j. *m.*, de Eilrico .v. *s.* pro fine .j. molendini.

Uxor Stephani de Bello Campo fuit filia Roberti Comitis de Ferrariis.

Marginal notes: d. d. d.[lii]

Hundredum de Lexeden'

174. Uxor Roberti de Stuteuill' est de donatione Domini Regis, et de parentela
Edwardi de Salesburia ex parte patris, et ex parte matris est de progenie Rogeri
de Reimes. Ipsa habet .j. villam que vocatur Diham, que est hereditas ejus, que

---

[lii] Only two notations are recorded in Round, *RD*, 69.

held it from Easter to 15 days after the next feast of Michaelmas.[211] In this period he took £10 from the farm of the vill, 5 marks and 20 rams from Robert de Beauchamp, 5 marks from Richard de Beauchamp, 20s from Geoffrey of Bedford, 3 marks and 2s 8d from Ernald, 2 marks and 2 pigs from Geoffrey, the reeve, 20s from Rimilda, the widow, 21s from William fitz Wimarc, one mark from William, the priest, half a mark from Robert fitz Goding, half a mark from Gilbert fitz Hoin, half a mark from Nicholas, 3s from Ralph Cristemesse, 3s from William de Stura, 3s from Nicholas Correui, and 8s from Ailric. The serjeants, Simon de Haspahal and Robert Barat, had 4s. The above Stephen had three daughters of whom the eldest is 14.[212] On Gilbert de Coleville's death the Lord King handed over the said land and the heir to Osbert Glanvill at the feast of St. Andrew.[213] When Gilbert de Coleville held the vill it was worth £11 per annum from the farm, with purchases, (but) without stock. And if it were stocked with 5 plough-teams, 2 harrow-beasts, 12 cows, one bull, 10 sows, one boar, and 100 sheep the vill would be worth £22 per annum, and it cannot sustain more stock nor be worth more, because the land is extremely infertile. Besides this vill Stephen held one carrucate of land in *Hald'eh'*, which he had as result of purchase, and he used to render rent from there, whose surplus is worth one mark of silver. In Fairstead, which is of the same fee, there is 7s 1½d from fixed rent, and one plough-team with 6 oxen and 2 horses, one harrow-beast, 2 cows, 2 sows, and 20 sheep, and it cannot be stocked with more; and with this stock it is worth 60s.[214] In Shenfield there is 8s in fixed rent, in Stratford 6s from fixed rent. From the same fee Osbert Glanvill took one mark from Ernald and 5s from Eilric as the fine for one mill. The widow of Stephen de Beauchamp was the daughter of Robert, earl of Ferrers.

(*Marginal notes*: d. d. d.)

Lexden Hundred

174. (Helewis), the widow of Robert de Stuteville, is in the Lord King's gift, and is from Edward of Salisbury's family on her father's side and Roger of Raimes' on her mother's.[215] She has one vill, which is called Dedham, which is her inheritance,

---

[211] 13 October 1184.

[212] According to no. 50 he had five daughters.

[213] 30 November 1184.

[214] This estate of Fairstead (*Fahistiam*) in Witham Hundred, Essex, is the same as that in no. 200.

[215] The family of Roger of Raimes is traced in Round, *Geoffrey de Mandeville*, appendix 10, 399–404. For Robert de Stuteville, see Clay, *Early Yorkshire Charters*, 9: 5–9, where five sons and two daughters are identified.

valet annuatim .xxiiij. *l.*; ipsa habet .j. filium et .ij. filias, et nescitur eorum etas a juratoribus.

Marginal note: d.

175. Willelmus de Lanuall' est in custodia Domini Regis, et habet totam terram suam, et nescitur a juratoribus quid valeat, nec etas ejus.

176. Gaufridus de Saukeuill' est in custodia Domini Regis, et Radulfus de Dena habuit custodiam .x. annis elapsis, et adhuc habet. Ipse habet in hundredo de Lexeden', Bures et Burcot', que valent .xxiij. *l.*, et non possunt plus valere. Etas ejus nescitur a juratoribus.

Marginal note: d.

Hundredum de Tendring'

177. Comitissa Juliana est de donatione Domini Regis, et est soror Comitis Albrici. Ipsa habet in hundredo de Tendring' .j. villam, scilicet, Duuercurt, que valet .xxx. *l.*, et Lexedene, que valet .x. *l.*, et est de feodo Comitis Albrici.

Marginal note: d.

178. Aliz de Tany est de donatione Domini Regis; terra ejus valet .vii. *l.*, et ipsa habet .v. filios et .ij. filias, et heres ejus est .xx. annorum, de progenie Rogeri de Reimes.

Hundredum de Heingford'

179. Filia Willelmi de Elint' est in custodia Domini Regis, et est .xv. annorum, et est neptis Parisii, archidiaconi. Stiestede, quam predictus Willelmus tenuit de monachis Cantuariensibus reddendo inde .x. *l.*, post mortem illius fuit in manu Domini Regis, cum filia ejusdem Willelmi, et in custodia vicecomitis Essex', qui primo anno inde recepit .iiij. *l.*, .iiij. *s.* minus; secundo anno .iiij. *m.* cum hoc

and it is worth £24 per annum. She has one son and two daughters, and their ages are not known by the jurors.

(*Marginal note*: d.)

175. William de Lanvaley is in ward to the Lord King and has all his land, and it is not known by the jurors what it is worth, nor his age.[216]

176. Geoffrey de Sauqueville is in ward to the Lord King and Ralph de Dene has had wardship for the past ten years and still does. He holds Bures and Bergholt in Lexden Hundred, which are worth £23, and they cannot be worth more. His age is not known by the jurors.

(*Marginal note*: d.)

Tendring Hundred

177. Countess Juliana[217] is in the Lord King's gift and is a sister of Earl Aubrey (de Vere, earl of Oxford). In Tendring Hundred she has one vill, viz. Dovercourt, which is worth £30, and Lexden, which is worth £10, and it belongs to the fee of Earl Aubrey.

(*Marginal note*: d.)

178. Alice de Tany is in the Lord King's gift. Her land is worth £7, and she has five sons and two daughters, and her heir is 20, and is descended from Roger de Raimes.[218]

Hinckford Hundred

179. The daughter of William of Allington is in ward to the Lord King and is 15; she is a niece of Paris, the archdeacon (of Rochester). Stisted, which the said William held of the monks of Canterbury by rendering £10 (per annum), was in the Lord King's hand after William's death, together with his daughter, and they are in the wardship of the sheriff of Essex. In the first year he received £3 16s from there, in the second year 4 marks, with the following stock: viz. 10

---

[216] Round, *RD*, 70, n. 2, identifies the property as Stanway in Lexden Hundred. For more on William de Lanvaley see nos. 107 and 201. His father had died in 1170: Amt, *The Accession of Henry II*, 76.

[217] Juliana de Vere, widow of Hugh Bigod, earl of Norfolk. The manor was not Lexden but rather Ingledesthorp, which was in Lexden Hundred: Round, *RD*, 71, n. 1.

[218] Her land was probably at Ardleigh in Tendring Hundred. See also nos. 174, 182, and 225.

instauramento, scilicet, .x. bobus, .v. equis; et si essent ibi .xvj. boves et .iiij. equi, et .vj. vacce et .j. taurus, .iiij. sues et .j. verris, et .lx. oves, dicta villa valeret .vj. *l.*, preter firmam monacorum, scilicet, .x. *l.*

180. Avicia de Liston', que fuit uxor Godefridi, camerarii, et filia Roberti de Liston', est in donatione Domini Regis, et terra ejus valet .xl. *s.*, et est hereditas ejus; et habet .j. filium, qui est .xxj. annorum; et ipsa debet facere canestellos, ad summonitionem, ad festum Regis.

Marginal note: d.

181. Avicia, que fuit uxor Nicolai de Stelbing' et filia Johannis de Mariny, est in donatione Domini Regis, et terra sua valet .ij. *m.*; et ipsa habet .ij. filios: primogenitus est .xij. annorum et in custodia Domini Regis, et per eum in custodia Petri Picot, et terra ipsius valet .iiij. *m.*

Marginal note: d.

182. Alicia, filia Willelmi filii Godcelin', quam [tradidit][liii] Dominus Rex Picoto de Tani, est in donatione Domini Regis, et tenet de Domino Rege, et de feodo Ricardi de Ramis; et terra sua valet .vii. *l.*; et ipsa habet .v. filios, et primogenitus est .xx. annorum, et .ij. filias. Picot de Tani habuit dictam terram .v. annis elapsis cum autumpnus venerit.

Marginal note: d.

183. Philippus de Danmartin, filius Philippi, est in custodia Domini Regis, et terra sua valet .lx. *s.*

Marginal note: d.

184. Willelmus, filius Willelmi de Curci, est in custodia Domini Regis, et per eum in custodia Roberti le Poher, et est .xx. annorum. Werefeld', terra sua, valet per annum .xx. *l.*; et dictus Robertus habuit custodiam jam .xv. annis.

[liii] "Tradidit" is suggested by Round, *RD*, 72, but it could equally have been "dedit," as, for example, in entries 28, 44, 52, 131, 192, and 227.

oxen and 5 horses; and if there were 16 oxen, 4 horses, 6 cows, one bull, 4 sows, one boar, and 60 sheep the said vill would be worth £6, besides the farm of the monks, viz. £10.[219]

180. Avice de Liston, widow of Godfrey, the chamberlain, and daughter of Robert de Liston, is in the Lord King's gift and her land is worth 40s, and it is her inheritance. She has one son who is 21. She is bound to make wafers on request at the Lord King's feast. [220]

(*Marginal note*: d.)

181. Avice, widow of Nicholas of Stebbing and daughter of John de Marney, is in the Lord King's gift and her land is worth 2 marks, and she has two sons; the eldest is 12 and is in ward to the Lord King, and through him in the wardship of Peter Picot, and his land is worth 4 marks.[221]

182. Alice, daughter of William fitz Jocelin, whom the Lord King gave in marriage to Picot de Tany, is in the Lord King's gift and she holds of the Lord King and of the fee of Richard de Raimes. Her land is worth £7, and she has five sons, of whom the eldest is 20, and two daughters. As of autumn Picot de Tany (would have) held the said land for the past 5 years. [222]

(*Marginal note*: d.)

183. Philip Daumartyn, son of Philip, is in ward to the Lord King and his land is worth 60s. [223]

(*Marginal note*: d.)

184. William fitz William de Courcy is in ward to the Lord King and through him is in the wardship of Robert le Poer. He is 20 years of age. His land of Wethersfield is worth £20 per annum, and Robert has had wardship now for 15 years.

---

[219] In the reign of Stephen Stisted was held at farm for £10 by Matilda of Saint-Saens (in Normandy) from the monks of Christ Church, Canterbury: *Regesta Anglo-Normannorum*, III, nos. 147–149. William of Allington's daughter was called Aveline and was later given in marriage to Osbert de Longchamp, a brother of the chancellor: Round, *RD*, 72, n. 1. Because she also held the serjeanty of Ovenhill she was a ward of the Crown, even though Stisted was not held in chief of the Crown. Cf. no. 170 and remarks on prerogative wardship.

[220] Her property was at Liston Overhall, Hinckford Hundred. The waferer serjeanty involved the making of wafers at major events such as the coronation and other crown-wearing occasions: Round, *The King's Serjeants*, 227–31.

[221] The unnamed manor was probably Porters Hall in Stebbing, Hinckford Hundred: Round, *RD*, 72, n. 2.

[222] Probably at Picotts in Saling, Hinckford Hundred: Round, *RD*, 72–73, n. 4. See no. 178: she is clearly the same Alice.

[223] The property was at Belchamp St. Ethelbert in Ovington, Hinckford Hundred: Round, *RD*, 73, n. 1.

Verumdictum de Rocheford

185. Filius Guidonis de Rocheford', scilicet, Johannes, est in custodia Domini Regis, et est .xvj. annorum, et habet fratrem .xij. annorum et sororem .xiiij. annorum. Rocheford' est terra ejus, que valeret annuatim .xij. *l.*, cum rationabili instauramento, quod totum ibi deficit. Et hoc potest ibi esse instauramenti, .vj. vacce, .j. taurus, .x. sues et .j. verris, .ij. carruce, .xij.ˣˣ·et .x. oves et .xxv. arietes. Et hoc precipitur instaurari. Custodes receperunt firma (*sic*) pasce .xvj. *s.*, de firma marisci ad Pascha .xviij. *s.*ˡⁱᵛ

Marginal note: Instaur'.

[Rot. 9. d.]

186. Beredene dimidia, que fuit Gwidonis de Rocheford', *cum una hida de feodo Comitis Willelmi, valet .xj. l. et .x. s.*ˡᵛ cum rationabili instauramento, scilicet, .ij. carrucis, .iiij. vaccis, .j. tauro, .v. suibus et .j. verre, et .lx. ovibus et .vj. arietibus, et precipitur instaurari. Custodes receperunt de firma .xiij. *s.*, et de fine cujusdam vidue .xx. *s.*

Marginal note: Instaur'.

Verumdictum de Hackeflete

187. Hackefleta valet annuatim .viij. *l.* cum rationabili instauramento, scilicet, .j. carruca et .ij. vaccis et .j. tauro, .xij.ˣˣ· ovibus et .xxiiij. arietibus et .j. herciorio. De hiis .viij. *l.* debent monachi de Monte Sancte Trinitatis habere .v. *m.* annuatim, et .v. *s.* de fine cujusdam femine.ˡᵛⁱ Ecclesia dicte ville est de donatione Domini Regis, quam Tomas Bardulf' dedit Henrico de Fontibus, cum mesagio et .xl. acris et .j. marisco de .xl. *s.*: et hoc postquam predicta Hackefleta fuit in manu Domini Regis. De catallis venditis habuit Henricus de Cornhill' .xl. *m.*, preter predictas

---

ˡⁱᵛ The words after ".xvi. *s.*" are struck out in the MS.

ˡᵛ The italicised section has been substituted for "valet annuatim .x. *l.*"

ˡᵛⁱ "Custodes receperunt .xxvi. *s.* de firma marisci" is struck out here.

The Testimony of Rochford [Hundred]

185. John, son of Guy de Rochford, is in ward to the Lord King and is 16, and he has a brother aged 12 and a sister aged 14. His land at Rochford would be worth £12 per annum with reasonable stock, which is not all there; and this is the stock that could be there: 6 cows, one bull, 10 sows, one boar, 2 plough-teams, 250 sheep, and 25 rams. It was ordered to be stocked. The custodians received 16s from the farm of the pasture, and 18s from the farm of the marsh at Easter.[224]

(*Marginal note*: to be stocked)

[Roll 9. dorse.]

(Clavering Hundred)

186. Half of Berden, which belonged to Guy de Rochford, together with one hide of the fee of Earl William (earl of Essex) is worth £11 10s with reasonable stock, viz. 2 plough-teams, 4 cows, one bull, 5 sows, one boar, 60 sheep, and 6 rams, and it was ordered to be stocked. The custodians received 13s from the farm and 20s from the fine of the same man's widow.

(*Marginal note*: to be stocked)

The Testimony of *Hackeflete*[225]

187. *Hackefleta* is worth £8 per annum with reasonable stock, viz. one plough-team, 2 cows, one bull, 240 sheep, 24 rams, and one beast for harrowing. From this £8 the monks of Mont Sainte-Trinité (Rouen)[226] ought to have 5 marks per annum and 5s from the fine of the same woman. The church of the said vill is in the Lord King's gift, which Thomas Bardulf gave to Henry de Fontibus with a messuage and 40 acres and one marsh worth 40s; and this was after *Hackefleta* came into the Lord King's hand. Apart from the above revenue Henry of Cornhill had 40 marks from the sale of chattels.[227] The widow of Guy de Rochford

---

[224] The 18s from the farm of the marsh has been struck out.

[225] According to Round, *RD*, 75, n. 2, this was in Dengey Hundred, a late twelfth-century renaming of Wibertsherne Hundred. It is argued that *Hackefleta* was the manor of Bradwell, whose advowson remained in the hands of the Bardulf family until 1403.

[226] Later known as Sainte-Trinité de Sainte-Catherine.

[227] This may be the 40 marks *de fine terre Widonis filii Widonis de Rocheford'* accounted for by Henry of Cornhill in *Pipe Roll 31 Henry II*, 44. The same entry includes payments to Mont St. Catherine of Rouen (5 marks), to the canons of St. Bartholomew, London (4s from Berden), and for the care of Guy de Rochford's sons (12 marks).

prisas. Uxor Guidonis de Rocheford fuit desponsata tempore Guidonis filii sui, et nescitur a juratoribus de cujus fuerit donatione, quia inde causa vertitur.

Verumdictum de Hundredo de Angre

188. Herebertus de Luci est in custodia Domini Regis, et per eum in custodia Godefridi de Luci. Terra ipsius de Stanford', cum pertinenciis, valet per annum .l. *l.* cum instauramento quod ibi habetur, scilicet, .viij. vaccis, et .xlvij. ovibus et .iiij. junioribus animalibus et .vj. carrucis et .v. porcis et .j. verre et .xx. hogastris; nec plus potest instauramenti pati. Instauramentum de Grenested' sunt .ii. carruce. Preter firmam recepit Godefridus de Luci, intra hos .iiij. annos, de dictis villis, .xv. *m.* Et preterea dictus Herebertus habet .c. solidatas terre in eodem hundredo, quas comes Glouecestr' dedit Ricardo de Luci; et hundredum, quod reddit .x. *m.* per annum. Herebertus de Luci est .xiiij. annorum.

Verumdictum de Estudeleford'

189. Comitissa de Ibernia est de donatione Domini Regis; filius ejus est in custodia Domini Regis, et est .xij. annorum. Cestreford', que est dos ejus, valet annuatim .xij. *l.* sine instauramento; et si esset instaurata de .ij. carrucis et .c. ovibus et .vj. vaccis et .j. tauro et .vij. porcis, ipsa valeret .xx. *l.*

190. Beatricia de Say est de donatione Domini Regis, et est .iiij.[xx.] annorum. Terra sua de Rikling' valet annuatim .xv. *l.* sine instauramento; et si esset instaurata de .ij. carrucis et .ii. vaccis et .j. tauro, et . . . . . . ovibus et .xx. porcis, dicta villa valeret annuatim .xx. *l.*

Verumdictum de Clavering

191. Alicia de Essex' est de donatione Domini Regis, et est .iiij.[xx.] annorum, et tenet Clavering sicut dotem suam de feodo Henrici de Essex. Et valet Clavering .xl. *l.* cum hoc instauramento, scilicet, .vj. carrucis, .c. ovibus, .iiij. vaccis et .j.

(re)married in the time of Guy, her son, and it is not known by the jurors in whose gift she was, because a lawsuit is pending concerning it.

The Testimony of Ongar Hundred

188. Herbert de Lucy is in ward to the Lord King and through him is in the wardship of Godfrey de Lucy.[228] His land of Stanford, with its appurtenances, is worth £50 per annum with the stock which is held there, viz. 8 cows, 47 sheep, 4 younger beasts, 6 plough-teams, 5 pigs, one boar, and 20 hoggets; nor is it possible to sustain more stock. The stock of Greensted amounts to 2 plough-teams. Besides the farm Godfrey de Lucy received 15 marks from the said vills these (past) 4 years. Furthermore, Herbert has 100 solidates of land in the same hundred, which the earl of Gloucester gave to Richard de Lucy,[229] together with the hundred, which returns 10 marks per annum. Herbert de Lucy is 14 years old.

The Testimony of East Uttlesford [Hundred]

189. The countess of Ireland is in the Lord King's gift.[230] Her son is in the Lord King's wardship and is 12 years of age. Chesterford, which is her dower, is worth £12 per annum without stock; and if it were stocked with 2 plough-teams, 100 sheep, 6 cows, one bull, and 7 pigs it would be worth £20.

190. Beatrice de Say is in the Lord King's gift and is 80.[231] Her land in Rickling is worth £15 per annum without stock; and if it were stocked with 2 plough-teams, 2 cows, one bull, . . . sheep, and 20 pigs it would be worth £20 per annum.

The Testimony of Clavering [Hundred]

191. Alice of Essex is in the Lord King's gift, is 80 years of age,[232] and holds Clavering as her dower of the fee of Henry of Essex. Clavering is worth £40 with the following stock: viz. 6 plough-teams, 100 sheep, 4 cows, one bull, 6 sows, one

---

[228] Godfrey de Lucy was Herbert's uncle and became bishop of Winchester in 1189.

[229] Richard de Lucy, chief justiciar under Stephen and Henry II, was Herbert's grandfather.

[230] See no. 168.

[231] Sister of Geoffrey de Mandeville, the first earl of Essex. See DeAragon, "Dowager Countesses," 94, and Johns, *Noblewomen*, 165, 174. Beatrice de Say was the grandmother of the Beatrice de Say who married Geoffrey fitz Peter: no. 115.

[232] In no. 61 she is recorded as 60 years of age. Her daughter is omitted from this entry.

tauro, .vj. suibus et .j. verre, et .ij. hercioriis. Dicta Alizia habet .ij. filios milites, et in comitatu Norhampton habet .xxx. libratas terre de feodo Comitis Willelmi.

192. Dominus Rex dedit filio Thome filii Bernard' filiam Walteri de Caune, cum Wanbrige, que valet annuatim .xx. *l.* cum pertinenciis; et ipsa est .v. annorum, et est in custodia uxoris que fuit Thome filii Bernard', post mortem ipsius Thome.

193. Agnes de Valuines est de donatione Domini Regis, et est .lx. annorum et eo amplius; et tenet Hecham et Leic', que valent annuatim .xiiij. *l.*

194. Margareta de Tony est de donatione Domini Regis, et est .lx. annorum; terra sua in Welcumestowe valet per annum .xxiiij. *l.*

Hundredum De Turst'

195. Willelmus, filius Galfridi de Tresgoz, est in custodia Domini Regis, et per eum in custodia Roberti de Luci, cujus filiam duxit in uxorem; et tenet de honore Peuerelli, et est .xvij. annorum. Terra sua de Toleshunt cum instauramento valet .xij. *l.*

Hundredum de Waltham

196. Uxor Turstini de Waltham est de donatione Domini Regis, et est .xxxvj. annorum, et habet .ij. filios et .ij. filias; primogenitus est .vj. annorum et dimidii; ipsa habet .j. carrucatam terre, et reddit inde .xiiij. *s.* annuatim Domino Regi. Ricardus filius Alcheri habet eam in custodia per Dominum Regem.

boar, and 2 harrow beasts. Alice has two sons who are knights, and in the county of Northampton she has 30 librates of land of the fee of Earl William.

(Wibertsherne Hundred)

192. The Lord King gave the daughter of Walter de Caune in marriage to a son of Thomas fitz Bernard, together with (North) Fambridge,[233] which, with its appurtenances, is worth £20 per annum. She is 5 and on Thomas fitz Bernard's death is in the wardship of his widow.[234]

(Becontree Hundred)

193. Agnes de Valoynes is in the Lord King's gift and she is more than 60. She holds Higham and Leyton, which are worth £14 per annum.[235]

194. Margaret de Toeni is in the Lord King's gift and is 60. Her land in Waltham-stow is worth £24 per annum.

Thurstable Hundred

195. William fitz Geoffrey de Tresgoz is in ward to the Lord King and through him is in the wardship of Robert de Lucy, whose daughter he married. He holds of the honour of Peverel and is 17. His land of Tolleshunt, with stock, is worth £12.[236]

Waltham Hundred

196. The widow of Turstin of Waltham is in the Lord King's gift and she is 36. She has two sons and two daughters. The elder son is six and a half. She has one carrucate of land and renders 14s per annum to the Lord King. Richard fitz Aucher has wardship of her through the Lord King.[237]

---

[233] South Fambridge was in Rochford Hundred, the other side of the River Crouch.

[234] This is an unusually early marriage. The three sons of Thomas fitz Bernard were aged 10, 8, and 3 (entry no. 227).

[235] For Agnes de Valoynes see also nos. 171 and 226.

[236] Another case of a custodian profiting from his office by the marriage of his daughter to the ward. See Round, *RD*, xxiv.

[237] Richard fitz Aucher was Turstin's brother: *Pipe Roll 30 Henry II*, 134.

Hundredum de Witham

197. Amabilia de Tresgoz est de donatione Domini Regis, et fuit filia Roberti Greslei, et habet filium Willelmum nomine, filium Galfridi de Tresgoz, et .iiij. filias. Filius ejus est in custodia Roberti de Luci, et fuit .viij. annis, et est .xvij. annorum. Predicta Mabilia tenet manerium de Dunteshale, quod valet .xij. *l.* et .xvij. *s.* cum instauramento quod potest pati, preter hoc quod inde reddit.

198. Eustacius, filius Willelmi de Howe, est in custodia Domini Regis, et Stephanus de Glanuill' habet inde custodiam. Dictus Eustacius [est] .xviij. annorum, et habet .j. fratrem et .ij. sorores. Terra sua de How valet .c. *s.* cum instauramento; et ipse [est] nepos H.^{lvii} vicecomitis Bolonie.

[Rot. 10.]

Secundus^{lviii} rotulus de Essex' de dominabus, pueris et puellis

199. Cristiana filia Willelmi filii Gerarard (*sic*) est de donatione Domini Regis, et est .xxv. annorum. Terra quam tenet de Rege valet .xx. *s.*; terra quam tenet de Gileberto Mauduit valet dim. *m.*: et ita tota terra valet .ij. *m.* Willelmus pater ejus fuit filius Gerardi Toci^{lix} de Hadfeld', de honore Peverelli, et ipsa fuit neptis Rogeri de Langeford'; et est seisita de terra sua, sed nescitur per quem.

200. Filius Stephani de Bello Campo est in custodia Domini Regis, et per eum in custodia Osberti de Glanvill', post mortem Gileberti de Coleuill', qui prius habuit custodiam, et est .iiij. annorum. Terra sua in Fairested' valet annuatim .lx. *s.*, que non potest plus valere.

---

^{lvii} A dot beneath the H probably indicates deletion.
^{lviii} ".ii." in MS.
^{lix} For "Coci."

Witham Hundred

197. Mabel de Tresgoz is in the Lord King's gift and was a daughter of Robert Grelley. She has a son called William fitz Geoffrey de Tresgoz, and four daughters. Her son, who is 17, is in the wardship of Robert de Lucy and has been for eight years. The aforesaid Mabel holds the manor of *Dunteshale*, which is worth £12 17s with stock which can be sustained, over and above that which she renders from there.[238]

198. Eustace fitz William of Hoo is in ward to the Lord King, and Stephen Glanvill has wardship there. Eustace is 18 years old and has one brother and two sisters. His land of Hoo[239] is worth 100s with stock; and he is a nephew of H. viscount of Boulogne.

[Roll 10.]

The second roll of Essex concerning ladies, boys, and girls

199. Christiana, daughter of William fitz Gerard, is in the Lord King's gift and is 25. Her land, which she holds of the Lord King, is worth 20s; the land which she holds of Gilbert Mauduit is worth half a mark; and so the total value is 2 marks.[240] William, her father, was a son of Gerard Toc of Hatfield, of the honour of Peverel, and she was a niece of Roger de Langford. She was put in possession of her land, but it is not known by whom.[241]

200. Stephen de Beauchamp's son is in ward to the Lord King and through him is in the wardship of Osbert Glanvill, after the death of Gilbert de Coleville, who held wardship previously; and he is 3 years old. His land in Fairstead is worth 60s per annum, and it cannot be worth more.[242]

---

[238] See no. 195. *Dunteshale* has been identified as the Tresgoz manor of Blunts Hall, Witham Hundred: Round, *RD*, 78, n. 4.

[239] Hoo Hall in Rivenhall, Witham Hundred.

[240] The land was probably at Hatfield Peverel in Witham hundred.

[241] The honour of Hatfield Peverel remained in royal control for most of the twelfth and thirteenth centuries: Sanders, *English Baronies*, 120.

[242] Cf. no. 173.

201. Willelmus de Lanuall' est in custodia Domini Regis, et est .lx. annorum, et habet terram suam in manu sua. Terra sua in Hallingeburia valet per annum .xvij. *l.*

202. Henricus de Valuines est in custodia Domini Regis, et per eum in custodia Hugonis de Morewich', et est .xviii. annorum. Terra sua in Salinges, tempore Willelmi de Vesci, solet esse ad firmam pro .xvij. *l.*, et ex illo tempore fuit ad firmam pro .xij. *l.* per annum.

203. Robertus, filius Roberti de Setvans, est in custodia Domini Regis, et per eum in custodia vicecomitis de Essex', et est .xij. annorum. Terra sua de Wigeberga fuit in manu Domini Regis elapso .j. anno a Piphania (*sic*). Malger et Ricardus receperunt inde firmam .ij. terminorum, scilicet, .xvij. *s.* ad Pascha, et todidem (*sic*) ad festum Sancti Michaelis. Postea commisit vicecomes terram illam Rogero, preposito, pro .xj. *l.*, cum .j. carruca de .vj. bobus, et .iiij. equis; et si essent ibi .ij. carruce, et .cc. oves et .viij. vacce et .xx. porcis (*sic*), tunc valeret terra. .xvj. *l.* Et precipitur instaurari. Et si terra de Colecestr' foret ei adjuncta, cum pertinenciis, et molendinum esset reparatum, dicta terra valeret per annum .xx. *l.*

(Harlow Hundred)

201. William de Lanvaley is in ward to the Lord King and is 60 years of age, and he is in possession of his own land. His land in (Great) Hallingbury is worth £17 per annum.[243]

(Hinckford Hundred)

202. Henry de Valoynes is in ward to the Lord King and through him in the wardship of Hugh de Morwich, and he is 18. His land in Saling was accustomed to be at farm for £17 in William de Vesci's time, and since then it has been at farm for £12 per annum.

(Winstree Hundred)

203. Robert, son of Robert de Setvans, is in ward to the Lord King and through him is in the wardship of the sheriff of Essex, and he is 12 years of age. His land in (Little) Wigborough has been in the Lord King's hand for a year since the Epiphany. Mauger and Richard received the farm of two terms there, viz. 17s at Easter and the same at Michaelmas. Afterwards the sheriff entrusted that land to Roger, the reeve, for £11,[244] with one plough-team of 6 oxen, and 4 horses; and if there were two plough-teams, 200 sheep, 8 cows, and 20 pigs the land would be worth £16. And it was ordered to be stocked.[245] And if the land of Colchester with its appurtenances were added and the mill repaired, the said land would be worth £20 per annum.

---

[243] As Round, *RD*, 80, n. 2, put it, there is something strange about William's age. No. 175 indicates that his age was unknown.

[244] This was the sum the sheriff accounted for at the Exchequer in 1185: *Pipe Roll 31 Henry II*, 14.

[245] The fact that it was subsequently fully stocked is shown in the following year's pipe roll, in which the sheriff of Essex accounted for the full £16. £8 10s was actually paid in, whilst allowances amounting to £7 10s were made for the purchase of 8 oxen (40s), 132 sheep (66s), 8 cows (24s), and subsistence for the heir (20s): *Pipe Roll 32 Henry II*, 12. This seems to be far better proof for the 1185 dating of the *Rotuli* than that provided by Round, *RD*, 42, n. 1.

204. Filius Willelmi filii Aluredi est in custodia Domini Regis, et per eum in custodia Henrici de Cornhill', et habet .ij. fratres et .iiij. sorores. Torindune, terra dicti Willelmi, fuit in manu dicti Henrici elapso .j. anno a festo Omnium Sanctorum, qui primo anno cepit inde .x. *s.*, et hoc anno .v. *s.* Dicta terra valet sine instauramento .l. *s.*, et cum instauramento .lv. [*s*].

Norhundredum de Chelmereford'

205. Filius Radulfi de Busseuill', qui tenet de honore Peuerelli, est in custodia Domini Regis, et per eum in custodia matris sue, et est .vij. annorum. Terra sua in Springefeld' valet per annum cum instauramento .viij. *l.*, quas mater ejus reddit Domino Regi.

206. Uxor que fuit Radulfi de Busseuill', que fuit filia Osberti filii Aucheri, est in donatione Domini Regis, et habet .ij. filios et .ij. filias, quorum primogenitus est .vij. annorum. Ipsa habet in Springefeld' .iiij. libratas terre in dote. Dicta villa valet annuatim .xij. *l.* cum instauramento .ij. carrucarum et .vj. vaccarum et .xl. ovium et .xx. porcorum.

Marginal note: d.[lx]

207. Cristiana de Ruilia est in donatione Domini Regis, et habet custodiam filii sui, qui est .xij. annorum, . . . [lxi] est hereditas ejus et valet annuatim .c. *s.*

Marginal note: d.[lxii]

[Rot. 10. d.]

208. Uxor que fuit Willelmi Granuel est in donatione Domini Regis; primogenitus filius ejus est .xviij. annorum, et ipsa habet feodum tertie partis unius militis; et ipsa fecit finem de custodia terre sue et filiorum suorum, et de relevio suo, pro .viij. *m.*

[lx] Omitted from Round, *RD*, 81.
[lxi] Blank in MS.
[lxii] Omitted from Round, *RD*, 81.

(Barstable Hundred)

204. The son of William fitz Alured is in ward to the Lord King and through him in the wardship of Henry of Cornhill,[246] and he has two brothers and four sisters. Horndon, William's land, was in the above Henry's hand for one year from the feast of All Saints, and he received in the first year 10s, and this year 5s. The said land is worth 50s without stock, and 55s with stock.[247]

North Hundred of Chelmsford

205. The son of Ralph de Boseville, who holds of the honour of Peverel, is in ward to the Lord King and through him is in the wardship of his mother, and he is 7 years old. His land in Springfield with stock is worth £8 per annum, which his mother pays to the Lord King.[248]

206. The widow of Ralph de Boseville, who was a daughter of Osbert fitz Aucher, is in the Lord King's gift and has two sons and two daughters; the firstborn son is 7. In Springfield she has 4 librates of land in dower. The said vill is worth £12 per annum with its stock of 2 plough-teams, 6 cows, 40 sheep, and 20 pigs.[249]

(*Marginal note*: d.)

207. Christiana de Ruilli is in the Lord King's gift and has wardship of her son, who is 12 . . .[250] is her inheritance and it is worth 100s per annum.

(*Marginal note*: d.)

[Roll 10. d.]

208. The widow of William Grenevilles is in the Lord King's gift. Her eldest son is 18 and she has one-third of a knight's fee, and she has paid a fine of 8 marks for the wardship of her own and her sons' land, and for her relief.[251]

---

[246] For Henry of Cornhill as custodian on other estates see nos. 170 and 187.

[247] See no. 211.

[248] In this year the sheriff accounted for £8 from the land of Ralph de Boseville: *Pipe Roll 31 Henry II*, 13.

[249] Nos. 205 and 206 present a very clear case of the mother taking wardship of the heir and his land, of retaining her dower worth one-third of the estate, and paying the dues from the remaining two-thirds to the Crown while the heir was still a ward of the Crown.

[250] Probably Great or Little Leigh in Chelmsford Hundred.

[251] Property unidentified.

209. Uxor que fuit Roberti, camerarii, est in donatione Domini Regis. Ipsa habet .iij. filios et .iiij. filias; primogenitus est de etate, et ipsa habet feodum unius militis, et filius habet terram suam.

210. Filius Roberti filii Odonis est in custodia Domini Regis, et est .vj. annorum, et ipse est heres decime partis unius militis, et vix possunt inde habere victum suum ipse et mater sua.

211. Thorindun' est in custodia Domini Regis cum herede, qui est .xix. annorum, que valet per annum .l. *s.* Ipse habet .iij. fratres et .iiij. sorores. Terra sua in Wakering valet .iiij. *l.* Terra sua in Berlesden' valet .ii. *m.* Ricardus filius Rogeri tenet .j. mariscum de eodem feodo, qui valet .xl. *s.* per annum.

212. Terra Walteri Anglici in Theia est in custodia Domini Regis cum herede, qui est unius anni. Terra illa valet .j. *m.* per annum.

[Rot. 11.]

Rotulus de viduis et puellis que sunt in donatione Domini Regis et de pueris qui sunt in ejus custodia in Cantebrigesire

Hundredum de Papewurthe

213. Mabilia, que est neptis Rannulfi de Glanuill', et in ejus custodia, fuit uxor Albrici Picot, et terra sua in Bukeswurthe est de feodo Gileberti de Muntfichet, et cum instauramento .j. carruce que ibi est, valet .xl. *s.*; et si ibi esset altera cum

209. The widow of Robert, the chamberlain,[252] is in the Lord King's gift. She has three sons and four daughters. The eldest son is of age, and she has one knight's fee, and her son is in possession of his land.[253]

210. The son of Robert fitz Odo is in ward to the Lord King and is 6 years old, and he is the heir to a tenth part of one knight's fee; and he and his mother are scarcely able to earn a living from it.[254]

211. Horndon is in the Lord King's wardship, together with its heir, who is 19, and it is worth 50s per annum. He has three brothers and four sisters.[255] His land in Wakering is worth £4. His land in Basildon is worth 2 marks.[256] Richard fitz Roger has one marsh of the same fee, which is worth 40s per annum.[257]

(Lexden Hundred)

212. The land of Walter Anglicus in Tey is in the Lord King's wardship, together with the heir, who is one year old. That land is worth one mark per annum.[258]

[Roll 11.]

Roll of ladies and girls who are in the Lord King's gift and of boys who in his wardship in Cambridgeshire

Papworth Hundred

213. Mabel, widow of Aubrey Picot and a niece of Rannulf Glanvill, is in the latter's wardship. Her land in Boxworth belongs to the fee of Gilbert de Mount-fitchet, and with stock of one plough-team, which is there, it is worth 40s (per

---

[252] Round, *RD*, 82, n. 1, suggests that by this time *Camerarius* indicates a surname rather than a profession. But the earlier entries recording *Camerarius* seem to indicate the profession: nos. 27, 67, 96, and 180.

[253] Property unidentified.

[254] Property unidentified.

[255] In entry no. 204, the son of William fitz Alured, the heir to Horndon, had two brothers and four sisters. The value, without stock, however, was the same, viz. 50s.

[256] Horndon and Basildon are in Barstable Hundred; Wakering is in Rochford Hundred.

[257] Cf. no. 187 where one marsh was also worth 40s per annum.

[258] Nos. 210 and 212 are examples of how minute some parcels of inheritance could be, especially serjeanties, but also those of petty knights.

.c. ovibus, que ibi esse possent, valeret .lx. et .x. *s.* Et ipsa est .lx. annorum et amplius, et habet .ij. filios et .iii. filias, et primogenitus est miles.

214. Due sorores in Papewurthe manent in helemosina Domini Regis, et debent pascere .j. pauperem propter Dominum Regem. Terra sua cum instauramento .j. carruce que ibi est, valet .xxx. *s.*; et si altera carruca cum .c. ovibus ibi esset, qui possent ibi esse, terra valeret .lx. *s.* Primogenita est .lx. annorum, et habet .iiij. filios et .ij. filias; altera est puella, et est .l. annorum, et sunt de progenie Gumeri de Stanton.

Marginal note: d.

Hundredum de Norstowe

215. Filius Albrici Picot, cum carrucata terre quam habet in Beche, est in custodia Rannulfi de Glanuill'.

Marginal note: d.[lxiii]

216. Comitissa Britannie, que est soror Regis Scottie, et de donatione Domini Regis, et habet in Barsingburn' de feodo comitis Britannie .xx. libratas terre, cum instauramento quod ibi est; et solet valere predictum manerium tempore Regis Henrici .xxvij. *l.* et .x. *s.* Ipsa est .xxx. annorum. Unam habet filiam, que est uxor comitis Britannie, et .j. filium[lxiv] habet de Humfrido de Buhun, qui est .x. annorum et in custodia Margarete de Buhun'.

Hundredum de Chileford'

217. Matildis de Ros, que fuit filia Ricardi de Kaunuill' et soror Gerardi de Kaunuill', est de donatione Domini Regis, et est .xl. annorum. Ipsa habet in Heldrikham .xij. libratas terre de feodo Gerardi de Kaunuill'; et ipsa habet de Willelmo de Ros .iij. filios et .iiij. filias. Primogenitus est .xx. annorum.

[lxiii] Omitted from Round, *RD*, 84.
[lxiv] Corrected from "filiam."

annum); and if there were another plough-team and 100 sheep, which there could be, it would be worth 70s. She is more than 60 years of age and has two sons and three daughters, and the elder son is a knight.

214. Two sisters reside in Papworth in alms of the Lord King and ought to support one pauper on the Lord King's behalf. Their land with stock of one plough-team, which is there, is worth 30s; and if there were another plough-team and 100 sheep, which there could be, the land would be worth 60s. The elder sister is 60 years old and has four sons and two daughters; the other is a maiden aged 50, and they belong to the family of Gumer of Stanton.

(*Marginal note*: d.)

Northstow Hundred

215. The son of Aubrey Picot with a carrucate of land in Waterbeach is in the wardship of Rannulf Glanvill.[259]

(*Marginal note*: d.)

(Armingford Hundred)

216. The countess of Brittany, sister of the King of Scotland, is in the Lord King's gift. In Bassingbourn of the fee of the count of Brittany she possesses 20 librates of land, with the existing stock. In the time of King Henry (I) the said manor was worth £27 10s. She is 30 years old.[260] She has one daughter, who is the wife of the count of Brittany, and a ten-year-old son by Humphrey de Bohun, who is in the wardship of Margaret de Bohun.

(Chilford Hundred)

217. Matilda de Ros, daughter of Richard de Camville and sister of Gerard de Camville, is in the Lord King's gift and is 40. She has 12 librates of land in Hildersham of the fee of Gerard de Camville. She has three sons and four daughters by William de Ros. The eldest son is 20 years of age.

---

[259] See no. 213.

[260] In earlier entries she is recorded as 40. See especially no. 160, where there are references to the same two children.

Hundredum de Werle

218. Sibilla de Harleton', que fuit filia Rogeri de Gigney, est de donatione Domini Regis, et .lxx. annorum et eo amplius. Ipsa habet in Herleton' de honore Comitis Giffard' .x. libratas terre. Rogerus de Huntingfeld' est ejus filius et heres, et preter illum, illa domina habet .ix. infantes.

219. Margareta de Muntfichet, que fuit filia Gileberti filii Ricardi de Clara, est de donatione Domini Regis, et est .lx. annorum et amplius. Gilebertus de Muntfichet est ejus filius et heres, et preter eum habuit .iij. infantes. Terra sua de Barenton' valet .xiij. *l.*; et si esset bene instaurata, valeret .xvj. *l.*

220. Juliana de Cathenis, que fuit filia Radulfi de Cathenis et uxor Ricardi del Estre, est de donatione Domini Regis. Terra sua in Berton' valet .iiij. *l.*, et bene instaurata valeret .c. *s.* et (*sic*), sed nescitur a juratoribus etas ejus, aut numerus puerorum.

Marginal note: d.[lxv]

221. Matillis Pecche, que fuit filia Hamonis Pecche, est de donatione Domini Regis, et habuit .xj. infantes de tribus maritis. Radulfus de Rouecestr' est heres ejus, et ipsa est .l. annorum. Terra sua in Haselingfeld' valet annuatim .viij. *l.* cum instauramento quod ibi est modo, scilicet, .xij. bobus, .iiij. averis, .v. vaccis, .j. tauro, .iij. vitulis, .lx. ovibus .j. minus, .xv. porcis; et si adderentur .ix.[es].xx. (*sic*) oves et .vii. averia et .j. herciorius (*sic*) et quinque porci et .j. verris, tunc valeret dicta terra .x. *l.*

Marginal note: d.[lxvi]

Hundredum De Trapelawe

222. Terra Margarete de Muntfichet in villa de Fulemere valet annuatim .xvj. *l.* cum instauramento presenti, scilicet, .ij. carrucis et .xl. ovibus; et bene instaurata, posset valere .xx. *l.*, scilicet, cum .iii. carrucis et ducentis ovibus et .xxj. porcis.

Marginal note: d.[lxvii]

[lxv] Omitted from Round, *RD,* 85.
[lxvi] Omitted from Round, *RD,* 86.
[lxvii] Omitted from Round, *RD,* 86.

Wetherley Hundred

218. Sybil of Harlton, daughter of Roger de Gigney, is in the Lord King's gift and is more than 70 years old. She has 10 librates of land in Harlton of the honour of Earl Giffard. Roger of Huntingfield is her son and heir, and besides him she has nine children.

219. Margaret de Mountfitchet, daughter of Gilbert fitz Richard de Clare, is in the Lord King's gift and is more than 60 years old. Gilbert de Mountfitchet is her son and heir, and besides him she had three children. Her land in Barrington is worth £13; and if it were well stocked it would be worth £16.[261]

220. Juliana of Keynes, widow of Richard del Estre and daughter of Ralph of Keynes, is in the Lord King's gift. Her land in Barton is worth £4, and well-stocked would be worth 100s. Her age is not known by the jurors, nor is the number of her children.

(*Marginal note*: d.)

221. Matilda Peche, who was the daughter of Hamo Peche, is in the Lord King's gift and had eleven children by three husbands. Ralph of Rochester is her heir, and she is 50. Her land in Haslingfield is worth £8 per annum with the existing stock, viz. 12 oxen, 4 farm-horses, 5 cows, one bull, 3 calves, 59 sheep, and 15 pigs; and if 180 sheep, 7 farm-horses, one harrow-beast, 5 pigs, and one boar were added then the said land would be worth £10.

(*Marginal note*: d.)

Thriplow Hundred

222. The land of Margaret de Mountfitchet in the vill of Fowlmere is worth £16 per annum with the present stock, viz. 2 plough-teams and 40 sheep; and well stocked, it could be worth £20, viz. with 3 plough-teams, 200 sheep, and 21 pigs.

(*Marginal note*: d.)

---

[261] See no. 222.

Aliud[lxviii] Hundredum

223. Filia Walteri de Bolebec est de donatione Domini Regis, et est .x. annorum. Villa de Swafham est de baronia Walteri de Bolebec, et filia ejus inde est heres, et data est in dotem uxori Gileberti Basset.

Marginal note: d.[lxix]

224. Terra Roberti Picot in Cueya, scilicet, fuodum (*sic*) .j. militis de Rege, et feodum alterius militis de episcopo Eliensi, est in custodia Rannulfi de Glanuill'; et Robertus Picot habet etatem, et est miles.

225. In villa de Wilbugeham dedit Dominus Rex .c. solidatas terre Picoto de Tany de dominio suo, et post mortem Picoti, Petrus frater ejus habuit custodiam terre et heredis per .iij. annos. Heres est .xx. annorum, et terra valet .c. *s.* cum hoc instauramento, scilicet, .c. ovibus et .j. carruca; sed quia nichil est instauramenti, reddunt firmarii annuatim .lx. *s.* Preter firmam cepit Petrus de relevio .xx. *s.* de quodam homine ejusdem feodi.

226. Agnes de Valuines, que fuit soror Pagani filii Johannis, est de donatione Domini Regis, et plusquam .lx[ta]. annorum. Ipsa habet in hundredo de Redefeld' quoddam manerium quod valet .xv. *l.* Filia ejus et heres data est Durando de Ostili.

227. Ewgenia Picot, que fuit filia Radulfi Picot de Kancia et uxor Thome filii Bernard', est de donatione Domini Regis, et est .xxx. annorum. Ipsa habet in hundredo de Redefeld' quoddam manerium quod valet annuatim .xxv. *l.*, et est de feodo Gileberti Malet; predictum manerium dedit Willelmus Malet predicte domine in dotem. Et ipsa habuit .iij. filios de Thoma filio Bernard', et .j. filiam: primogenitus est .x. annorum, medius .viij. annorum, tertius trium annorum. Filiam dedit Dominus Rex filio Johannis de Bidun.

[Rot. 11. d.]

Endorsed: Primi rotuli de Cantebrigg' de dominabus.[lxx]

[lxviii] MS: "Alid."

[lxix] Omitted from Round, *RD*, 86.

[lxx] This suggests that there was another roll for Cambridgeshire.

Another Hundred (Staine Hundred)

223. The daughter of Walter of Bolbec is in the Lord King's gift and is 10 years of age. The vill of Swaffham belongs to the barony of Walter of Bolbec, and his daughter is heir there, and it (Swaffham) was given in dower to the wife of Gilbert Basset.[262]

(*Marginal note*: d.)

224. The land of Robert Picot in Quy, viz. one knight's fee of the King and another knight's fee of the bishop of Ely, is in the wardship of Rannulf Glanvill; and Robert Picot is of age and is a knight.[263]

225. In the vill of Wilbraham the Lord King gave 100 solidates of land to Picot de Tany from his (royal) demesne, and after Picot's death his brother Peter had wardship of the land and its heir for three years. The heir is 20 years of age and the land is worth 100s with the following stock, viz. 100 sheep and one plough-team, but because there is no stock there the farmers render 60s per annum. Besides the farm Peter took 20s in relief money from a certain man of the same fee.[264]

(Radfield Hundred)

226. Agnes de Valoynes, who was the sister of Payn fitz John, is in the Lord King's gift and is more than 60 years old. In Radfield Hundred she has a certain manor, which is worth £15. Her daughter and heir was married to Durand de Osteill.[265]

227. Eugenia Picot, daughter of Ralph Picot of Kent and widow of Thomas fitz Bernard, is in the Lord King's gift and she is 30. She has a certain manor in Radfield Hundred, which is worth £25 per annum and belongs to the fee of Gilbert Malet. William Malet gave the said manor to this lady in dower. She had three sons and one daughter by Thomas fitz Bernard. The eldest son is 10 years old, the second 8 years, and the third 3 years. The Lord King gave the daughter in marriage to the son of John de Bidun.[266]

Endorsed: of the first roll for Cambridgeshire concerning ladies

---

[262] See no. 71, in which Walter of Bolbec's daughter was reckoned to be 9 at Michaelmas 1184. Walter of Bolbec's widow was presumably given in marriage to Gilbert Basset.

[263] See nos. 213 and 215.

[264] See nos. 178 and 182. The son and heir was Ralph Picot: *Pipe Roll 30 Henry II*, 10.

[265] Agnes is the same age in no. 193, but given as 50 in no. 171. According to Round, *RD*, 87, n. 2, it was her granddaughter who married Durand.

[266] This was undoubtedly another very young marriage. See no. 192 for a betrothal, if not marriage, at the age of five, and no. 114, where Matilda, wife of John de Bidun and daughter of Thomas fitz Bernard, is recorded as widowed at the age of 10. See Johns, *Noblewomen*, 184.

Rotulus de dominabus de Midelsex'

[Rot. 12.]

228. Hawis de Windesor' est de donatione Domini Regis, et habet .j. filium, qui est .xviij. annorum, et .vj. filias. Terra sua in Stamwell' valet .c. *s.*: et preterea in hoc comitatu habet tres milites fefatos.

[Roll 12.]

Roll concerning ladies of Middlesex

(Spelthorne Hundred)

228. Hawise of Windsor is in the Lord King's gift and has one son, who is 18, and six daughters. Her land in Stanwell is worth 100s. Furthermore, in this shire (Middlesex) she has three enfeoffed knights.[267]

---

[267] The three Middlesex knights' fees were in Stanwell, Bedfont, and Poyle (in Stanwell): Round, *RD*, 88, n. 1. See nos. 73 and 87.

SELECT BIBLIOGRAPY

Amt, E. *Women's Lives in Medieval Europe: A Sourcebook*. New York, 1993.

———. *The Accession of Henry II in England: Royal Government Restored 1149-1159*. Cambridge, 1993

Bartlett, R. *England under the Norman and Angevin Kings, 1075-1225*. Oxford, 2000.

Chibnall, A. C. *Sherington: Fiefs and Fields of a Buckinghamshire Village*. Cambridge, 1965.

Clark, J. W., ed. *Liber Memorandorum Ecclesie de Bernewelle*. Cambridge, 1907.

Clay, C. T., ed. *Early Yorkshire Charters*. 10 vols. Wakefield, 1939-1955.

Cockayne, G. E. *Complete Peerage*. 14 vols. London, 1910-1998.

Coss, P. *The Lady in Medieval England*. Stroud, 1998.

Crook, D., ed. *Records of the General Eyre*. Public Record Office Handbook 20. London, 1982.

DeAragon, R. C. "Dowager Countesses, 1069-1230," *Anglo-Norman Studies* 17 (1995): 87-100.

D'Ewes, Simonds, and Dodsworth, R. *Historica Monumenta Diversa*. London, 1643.

Domesday Book: Text and Translation, ed. J. Morris. 35 vols. Chichester, 1975-1986.

Douglas, D. C. *The Social Structure of Medieval East Anglia*. Oxford, 1927.

———, and Greenaway, G. W., eds. *English Historical Documents 1042-1189*. London, 1968.

Farmer, D. L. "Prices and Wages." In *The Agrarian History of England and Wales*, ed. J. Thirsk, 2: 715-817. Cambridge, 1988.

Foulds, T. ed. The Thurgarton Cartulary. Stamford, 1994.

Grimaldi, S., ed. *Rotuli de Dominabus et Pueris et Puellis de Donatione Regis in XII Comitatibus*. London, 1930.

Hallam, H. E. "Farming Techniques: Eastern England." In *The Agrarian History of England and Wales*, ed. Thirsk, 2: 272-312.

Harvey, S. "Taxation and the Ploughland in Domesday Book." In P. H. Sawyer, ed., *Domesday Book: a Reassessment*, 86-103. London, 1985.

Herlihy, D. *Medieval Households*. Cambridge, MA, 1985.

Johns, S. M. *Noblewomen, Aristocracy and Power in the Twelfth-Century Anglo-Norman Realm*. New York and Manchester, 2003.

Lally, J. E. "Secular Patronage at the Court of Henry II." *Bulletin of the Institute of Historical Research* 49 (1976): 159-84.

Moore, J. S. "The Anglo-Norman Family: Size and Structure." *Anglo-Norman Studies* 14 (1992): 153-96.

Loengard, J. S. " 'Of the Gift of Her Husband': English Dower and its Consequences in the Year 1200." In J. Kirshner and S. F. Wemple, eds., *Women of the Medieval World*, 215-55. Oxford, 1985.

Mortimer, R. "The Family of Rannulf Glanville." *Bulletin of the Institute of Historical Research* 54 (1981): 1-16.

Mortimer, R. *Angevin England 1154-1258*. Oxford, 1994.

Pipe Rolls, published by the Pipe Roll Society, cited by regnal year of the king.

Poole, A. L. *From Domesday Book to Magna Carta*. 2nd ed. Oxford, 1955.

Reedy, W. T., ed. *Basset Charters c. 1120-1250*. Pipe Roll Society, 88, n.s. 1. London, 1995.

Round, J. H. Geoffrey de Mandeville. London, 1892.

———. *The King's Serjeants and Officers of State*. London, 1911.

———, ed. *Rotuli de Dominabus et Pueris et Puellis de XII Comitatibus*. Pipe Roll Society 35. London, 1913.

———. *Feudal England*. London, 1964.

Sanders, I. J. *English Baronies*. Oxford, 1960.

Stafford, P., and Labarge, M. W. "Women." In *Medieval England: An Encyclopedia*, ed. P. E. Szarmach et al., 807-10. New York, 1998.

Thirsk, J. ed., *The Agrarian History of England and Wales*, vol. 2, 1042-1350. Cambridge, 1988.

Turner, R. V. "The Mandeville Inheritance, 1189-1236: Its Legal, Political and Social Context." *Haskins Society Journal* 1 (1989): 147-72.

Van Houts, E. *Memory and Gender in Medieval Europe*. London, 1999.

Victoria County History, volumes for the twelve counties.

Warren, W. L. *Henry II*. Berkeley, 1973.

Ward, J. *Women of the English Nobility and Gentry*. Manchester, 1995.

INDEX NOMINUM ET LOCORUM

For both indexes the numbering is by entry rather than by page
Abbreviations: cust, custodian; Hd, Hundred; Wap, Wapentake

INDEX RERUM